Divination for Beginners

Unlocking Future Prediction Methods of Astrology, Tarot, Numerology, Palm Reading, Crystals, Runes, and Crystal Balls

© Copyright 2023 - All rights reserved.

The content contained within this book may not be reproduced, duplicated, or transmitted without direct written permission from the author or the publisher.

Under no circumstances will any blame or legal responsibility be held against the publisher, or author, for any damages, reparation, or monetary loss due to the information contained within this book, either directly or indirectly.

Legal Notice:

This book is copyright protected. It is only for personal use. You cannot amend, distribute, sell, use, quote, or paraphrase any part, or the content within this book, without the consent of the author or publisher.

Disclaimer Notice:

Please note the information contained within this document is for educational and entertainment purposes only. All effort has been executed to present accurate, up-to-date, reliable, and complete information. No warranties of any kind are declared or implied. Readers acknowledge that the author is not engaging in the rendering of legal, financial, medical, or professional advice. The content within this book has been derived from various sources. Please consult a licensed professional before attempting any techniques outlined in this book.

By reading this document, the reader agrees that under no circumstances is the author responsible for any losses, direct or indirect, that are incurred as a result of the use of the information contained within this document, including, but not limited to, errors, omissions, or inaccuracies.

Free Bonus from Silvia Hill available for limited time

Hi Spirituality Lovers!

My name is Silvia Hill, and first off, I want to THANK YOU for reading my book.

Now you have a chance to join my exclusive spirituality email list so you can get the ebooks below for free as well as the potential to get more spirituality ebooks for free! Simply click the link below to join.

P.S. Remember that it's 100% free to join the list.

~~$27~~ FREE BONUSES

-  9 Types of Spirit Guides and How to Connect to Them
-  How to Develop Your Intuition: 7 Secrets for Psychic Development and Tarot Reading
- 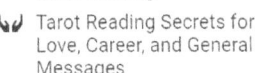 Tarot Reading Secrets for Love, Career, and General Messages

Access your free bonuses here
https://livetolearn.lpages.co/divination-for-beginners/

Table of Contents

INTRODUCTION 1
CHAPTER 1: DIVINATION NOW AND THEN 3
CHAPTER 2: ASTROLOGY AND DIVINATION 13
CHAPTER 3: DECODING YOUR BIRTH CHART 24
CHAPTER 4: NUMEROLOGY 34
CHAPTER 5: YOUR LIFE PATH NUMBER 43
CHAPTER 6: THE DIVINING ART OF TAROT 52
CHAPTER 7: HOW TO READ THE TAROT 62
CHAPTER 8: PALMISTRY AND PALM READING 72
CHAPTER 9: RUNIC DIVINATION 82
CHAPTER 10: CRYSTAL DIVINATION 93
BONUS: GLOSSARY OF TERMS 102
CONCLUSION 109
HERE'S ANOTHER BOOK BY SILVIA HILL THAT YOU MIGHT LIKE 111
FREE BONUS FROM SILVIA HILL AVAILABLE FOR LIMITED TIME 112
REFERENCES 113

Introduction

Divination is an age-old method used to gain insight into situations, events, and connections made in the future. No divination method will tell you the exact future. The answers revealed are all subject to interpretation. And there are different techniques designed to gather knowledge about future happenings, but they can only serve as an inspiration. Interpreting the future means looking into something that is constantly changing. No event is fixed - and this is mainly due to free will.

You can ask for a specific answer, but how you interpret it and how it will come to reality are two different things. Your thoughts and actions at the time of reading will influence how you map out your future and whether the results you predict come true. No matter how clearly you see the picture of your future, the outcome can change as soon as you change any aspect of your behavior. And you're free to change your mind anytime you want to.

Since the beginning of time, there have been examples of divination in many different cultures. Some of these practices started as simple observations of events happening on Earth. Other cultures went beyond observing, fashioning tools with the specific intent of discerning what the future holds for them. In either case, the energy of the diviner carries the primary influence alongside the universal energy of life. When divination is done for another person, their energy will mix these forces and provide answers in one form or another.

Another crucial aspect of divination is the question you'll be asking. The type of answers you're interested in will also influence which divinatory method is the best to answer your specific question. You may feel that a particular technique provides you with better insight into critical questions about your life's potential. Some also find it easier to collect energy by using specific tools, which facilitate the revelation of the answers they are looking for. The questions and their answers also need to reflect your situation. Although suitable for beginners, "yes" or "no" questions won't reveal much about the future. They can only confirm something but not how it comes to be. When asking more open-ended questions, you'll be more likely to access the pool of available information about any area of life you want to know about.

This thorough and practical guide provides all the tools you need to discover your future. It is a perfect stepping stone for those wanting to delve into divinatory practices like astrology, tarot, numerology, chiromancy, palmistry, and runic divination. Just as these art forms gave answers to ancient civilizations, they will provide you with information about the past, present, and future in the same way. Whether you're just looking to find the perfect technique or are a skilled practitioner seeking to reconnect with a specific divinatory form, you'll find the way to do so throughout this book.

Whichever method you choose to add to your practices, the key to mastering it will be working on your intuition. After all, the answers you receive can only be interpreted correctly if you recognize whether they align with your values. In most cases, this is the first meaning that comes to mind, as this is the closest one to your true self. If you're ready to explore which divinatory art resonates with your values and personality, read on, and you'll find out.

Chapter 1: Divination Now and Then

Divination is one of the most interesting yet little-known magical practices today. When people think of divination, they generally think of Harry Potter, Professor Trewlaney, crystal balls, and reading tea leaves. While Harry Potter has undoubtedly brought the practice of divination to widespread notice, there's far more to this practice than is to be found in the books and movies.

Divination is widespread and found worldwide.
https://www.pexels.com/photo/woman-in-red-hat-and-black-outfit-sitting-on-the-bed-while-holding-a-crystal-ball-6806745/

Divination is essentially an attempt to improve our insight into questions and situations that don't have a clear solution. Today, it is generally considered an attempt to foretell the future. However, there's more to divination than simply reading and predicting the future.

This book details and helps you understand divination, as well as introduces you to how it is best practiced. However, before you can do that, understanding its history will give you a solid base of knowledge to work from.

History of Divination

Divination was known to have been practiced as far back as the ancient Greeks and Romans. In ancient Greece, oracles were held in high respect and were considered to be a link between the gods and humans. In fact, the divinatory revelations of the oracles were considered to have literally been words from the gods.

Indeed, oracles were in high demand. However, their divinatory revelations were so rare that getting a prediction from an oracle became a valued commodity in ancient Greece.

Oracles were not the only vessels of divination in ancient Greece, nor were they the most common. Seers filled this role.

Unlike oracles, seers did not speak the words of the gods directly, and contrary to their name, they did not "see" the future. Rather, they read and interpreted signs offered by the gods using methods such as reading the entrails of animals that had been ritually sacrificed and reading the signs of the birds. Seers, unlike oracles, could only answer yes or no questions.

Seers were so essential to life in ancient Greece and Rome that they were often found on battlegrounds and in army camps, as generals would need to consult with them on battlefield tactics. Without the seer's approval (through the reading of certain signs), battles would not occur.

It should be noted that seers and oracles were not just common among the Greeks and Romans. They were also popular among the ancient Egyptians. One of the best-known mentions of an oracle and divination in antiquity is Alexander the Great's meeting with the Oracle of Amun at the Siwa Oasis.

While belief in divination dates back to antiquity, so does skepticism of the practice. Given the influence and power the seers and oracles held, many people were skeptical about the veracity of their claims. However, more people actually believed in their abilities. But, as years passed, there was a growing distrust in oracles which led to a decline in their popularity and use by the 1st century AD. Various forms of divination were practiced throughout the world, including astrology in India and the Middle and Near East and in Kabbalah by the Jews. In China, the I Ching (also known as the Yi Jing) is one of the oldest known divinatory texts and explores cleromancy, a form of divination also known as I Ching divination. This complex form of divination involves the use of yarrow stalks.

Divination can be practiced using instruments, as in I Ching divination, or through bodies, such as the divination of the Greek oracles. The practice is widespread and found worldwide.

Divination in the Middle Ages

While divination is carried out throughout the world, the prohibition of the craft found in some books of the Bible, combined with the growing popularity of Christianity, led to a decline in public popularity. People practicing forms of divination were often prosecuted and even put to death. One example is the Electorate of Saxony, whose laws from 1572 to 1661 say that it is against the law to tell the future, and the penalty is death.

At the same time, folk practitioners kept traditional versions of divination alive. While they were often punishable by death, they were just as often practiced. They were especially popular with people in the lower social classes.

Nonetheless, divination continued to be practiced in non-European countries. For example, Islamic countries promoted the study of astrology at a state level. Additionally, geomancy (divination with sand, rocks, or soil) was popular with people of all social classes and was used to divine prophecies.

Different forms of divination that were popular in Islamic countries included oneiromancy, or divination through dream interpretation, and the uniquely Islamic "science of letters," which involved the study of the Koran combined with mathematics.

In other parts of the world, Islamic divination involved the intervention of religious leaders, healers, and dedicated diviners. It also involved items like amulets. In fact, in West Africa, Islamic diviners were crucial to helping spread Islam around the continent.

The practice of divination also continued in Mesoamerica, with divinatory practices including scrying through mirrors, casting lots, and using kernels of maize to divine answers.

Divination Today

Today has seen a re-awakening of interest in the Western world. It is practiced as part of a variety of esoteric religious practices, including:

- Wicca
- Paganism
- Witchcraft
- Voodoo
- Santeria

Each religion has its own tools. Some, like Wicca, paganism, and witchcraft, use many different items as their divinatory tools.

In parts of India and Nepal, oracles who channel the gods in their bodies can still be found.

In Japan, divination involves traditional and foreign forms of divination, like Onmyōdō, I Ching divination, and tarot reading. The Chinese zodiac signs, cardinal directions, four elements, yin-yang, and planets all play key roles in modern Japanese divination. Tarot cards are so popular that there are multiple decks designed with Japanese culture in mind.

In Taiwan, Poe, or mood board divination (using two wooden blocks shaped like crescent moons), continues to be used. At the same time, the followers of the Serer religion in Senegal believe in hereditary rain priests who are believed to be able to divine the future.

Aside from "religious" divination, fortune-telling apps, websites, and individuals will offer to tell a person's fortune as a form of entertainment at carnivals and fairs. Today, the future is available to everyone who seeks it. However, these "gimmick divinations" are far less reliable and more generic than the answers offered through regular divinatory practice.

The desire to learn more about things to come is part of human nature, and as long as this desire remains a driving force behind our actions, divination will continue to play an important role worldwide.

How Divination Works

When people think of divination, they think of predictions of the future. Specifically, they think of it as forecasting and telling the future.

However, this is not the only thing that divination can do. Depending on the type of tradition of divination, it can also be diagnostic, a way to find answers to questions, advice, and guidelines to follow, as well as interventionist – that is, a way to intervene in an undesired potential future.

This is part of the reason divination is so popular. Not only does it tell the future, but some traditions also allow people to use this knowledge to change the future.

Keep in mind that this is not always possible. For example, Greek mythology is full of references to stories of people who heard unfortunate prophecies from the oracles and tried to subvert the future, such as Perseus's grandfather and Oedipus's father, only to end up being the cause of the prophecy coming true.

However, in many traditions, divination is seen as more of an insight into potential or a future that may potentially come true unless acted upon. This allows the person whose future is "being read" to determine whether it is something they wish to act on or not. Destiny is not an immutable law but can be changed depending on a person's actions, and divination gives a person a chance to be the author of those changes.

It should also be noted that divination is a living and constantly changing practice. People choose to interpret symbols differently, and existing symbols gain new meanings over time. Because divination often involves interpretation, reading for one person, and answering the same question, it may differ from one diviner to the next. This isn't to say that either is wrong – only that each provides a different perspective to the answer.

Types of Divination

As discussed, there are numerous divination traditions followed around the world. Many forms that fell out of favor due to religious persecution and witch hunts have, in the past 100 years or so, been gaining popularity again.

Given that there are hundreds of types of divination, listing them all is impossible. However, here are some of the most common forms of those practiced today and those which were more evident in the past:

Tarot Cards

Reading Tarot cards (also known as tarotmancy) involves much interpretation. While it seems like Tarot readers are "reading the future," they simply provide an interpretation of the most probable outcome defined by the cards. Tarot cards do not provide perfect insights into a person's future. In most cases, your future, as defined by the cards, is perpetually in flux and changeable.

Tarot is best regarded as a divinatory tool for self-improvement and reflection, providing you with a guide you can use to alter your life if need be.

Celtic Ogham

Also known as Ogham casting, this is a form of cleromancy. It involves using the Celtic Ogham alphabet carved on staves (or short sticks), casting them, then interpreting the patterns formed by how the staves fall.

Norse Runes

Also known as rune casting involves carving the Norse runes onto rocks, pebbles, or, traditionally, wood (one rune to a chosen material) and then casting them on a white linen sheet. Depending on how the runes land, divinatory interpretations are made.

Tasseomancy

Tasseomancy involves reading tea leaves or coffee grounds, though the former is more common. Tasseomancy is a good example of the living nature of divinatory. This is a relatively new divinatory practice that started in the 17th century.

You cannot do a tea reading without first having the leaves to read. Brew up a cup of tea with loose leaves; *do not remove* the leaves from the cup. Instead, let them settle at the bottom of the cup and then drink the tea until only the leaves are left. When only the wet leaves are left, give them a swirl until you see patterns emerge – this is when you can start to read.

Pallomancy

Pallomancy is one of the easiest forms of divination and involves using a pendulum. You can usually only ask yes or no questions for this form of divination, but it is a good introduction to the world of divinatory practices.

Pendulums are often used in conjunction with pendulum boards, tarot cards, and other magical tools. Some people even use a pendulum as a kind of dowsing rod.

Astrology

Also known as astromancy, this form of divination involves reading the movements and position of the planets, stars, and other celestial bodies. One of the most popular forms of astrology is drawing up and reading a person's birth chart, which is a comprehensive chart showing how each relevant celestial body was positioned in the night sky at the time of a person's birth.

There are different forms of astrology readings, depending on the purpose of the person's question. For example, some forms include horoscopic and natal astrology, electional astrology, sun sign astrology, and locational astrology. There are also different astrological traditions worldwide, including Indian astrology, Hellenistic astrology, Chinese astrology, and Western astrology.

Numerology

Numerology is a divinatory practice where those using it believe numbers hold enormous significance. Numerology involves studying the mystical relationships between numbers and how numbers affect events. Some numerical combinations are considered more potent and can be applied to different situations. For example, they may act as a reference to how a person should change their name.

Various numeric systems are used in numerological divination, including Pythagorean, Chaldean, Agrippan, and Kabbalistic. It can also be combined with astrology for a more informed insight into questions.

Palmistry

Also known as palm reading, this practice is about finding answers by studying a person's palm. There are many variations of this worldwide practice, which is popular in:

India and the Indian sub-continent

Persia

Sumeria

Greece

The Catholic Church banned the practice, and there were two papal edicts against it enforced by Popes Paul IV & Sixtus V.

This technique involves reading the lines on a person's palm and using them to make predictions. While palmistry has declined in popularity in the West, it remains enormously popular in other parts of the world, particularly in South and South-East Asian countries.

Crystal Divination

As its name suggests, Crystal divination uses crystals to make divinatory predictions. One of the most popular forms of crystal divination is crystal scrying or crystal ball reading, which involves looking at a crystal ball to see visions of the future.

Other types of crystal divination include crystal throwing. This is done by filling a pouch with stones, crystals, and gemstones and throwing them onto a premade grid. Predictions are made depending on where each stone falls on this grid.

You can either make your own personalized grid at home or find a pattern online.

Osteomancy

Osteomancy is about finding answers in the bones of animals or humans. The traditions of osteomancy differ around the world, and the bones are prepared in different ways, including:

Ceremonially burning them

Marking them with magical symbols

Mixing them in a pouch with other items

In the past, animals were often sacrificed specifically to use their bones for osteomancy. This rarely happens today, and it is common to use animal bones from animals that have died from natural causes or accidents.

Geomancy

Stones and socks can show patterns when they are cast together. You'll find patterns when casting smaller materials like soil and sand. These patterns can be read by those who know what to look for. It was common around Europe and Africa and was also particularly popular in Islamic countries.

Hydromancy

Where geomancy uses sand and soil for divination, hydromancy uses water for the same purposes. Some elements interpreted in a search for answers include the following elements:

Color.

Ripples.

The ebb and flow of disturbed water.

Lithomancy

Lithomancy involves using stones to tell the future. This form of divination has been around for thousands of years and can be traced back to the Bronze Age.

To perform lithomancy, stones are carved/painted with symbolic designs before being cast. The way the stones fall is interpreted to answer your questions. In some lithomantic traditions, diviners read the way that light reflects off the stones. In these traditions, colored glass stones are generally used instead of natural stones.

These are only some of the many forms of divination. Given the popularity of their form of magic, there are hundreds of variations of divination in the world. Some have their own sub-techniques and variations, which creates a potential list of thousands of divinatory traditions worldwide.

While mastering all forms is not possible, it is possible to choose the one which speaks to you the most – *and master it*. This book will help you explore astrology, numerology, palmistry, runic divination, Tarot card reading, and crystal divination in further detail.

Firstly, it will look at how astrology connects to divination and help you to understand what birth charts are and how you can make your own. Next, you'll learn about numerology and your life path number.

You'll then read about the Tarot, including an introduction to the cards and how to read them. Finally, the book will look at the following:

Palmistry

Runic divination

And crystal divination in further detail

By the time you have finished reading the book, you'll have a better idea of which of these relatively popular forms of divination speak to you most and which you'd like to explore further. You'll be able to make an educated decision on which form of divination to concentrate your abilities on.

So, what are you waiting for? All that's left for you is to turn the page and continue reading!

Chapter 2: Astrology and Divination

Astrology has been used for divination since the beginning of time. Several ancient cultures observed the positions of celestial bodies and associated their placings and movements with corresponding events that took place on Earth. Nowadays, while surrounded by many misconceptions, astrology is still one of the most popular methods for determining people's life paths. This chapter discusses the concept of astrology, its relation to astronomy, and how best to use it for divination.

The True Concept of Astrology

Astrology can be defined as a reflection of the connection between the activity of heavenly bodies and events surrounding people's lives on Earth. Astrologers study how planetary bodies affect one's career, health, and relationships. The latter can simultaneously be applied to more than one person, allowing the astrologer to analyze compatibility within a relationship. They can also predict how current global events, financial markets, social trends, and localized disasters are influenced by celestial movements. Because this is based on the movement of the planetary bodies within a specific timeframe, in-depth reports are usually generated weekly or monthly. However, astrology can also help predict more generalized pictures, which indicate possible future outcomes of one's actions.

This is based on the placement of the planets at the time you were born.

While each celestial body has its own purpose in astrology, depending on the specific use of the reading, some are more significant than others. For example, personal readings always look at the position and the movements of the sun and the moon first, and then the other planets. This is because your sun sign determines your core identity while the rest of the celestial bodies influence smaller nuances of your personality and life. For a monthly report (used for horoscopes), astrologers only look at the zodiac sign a celestial body is currently moving through. They represent the final aspect of your personality. Together with the zodiac houses, they influence how your core personality is expressed.

Astrological Disciplines

There are more than 80 branches of astrology, each employing different practices, purposes, and subsets of techniques. However, most of them can be filed into one of the following categories.

Natal Astrology

As the most popular form of divination, natal astrology is based on the position of the major heavenly bodies at the time and date of your birth. This report is called the natal chart, a testimony to your predicted life path. It can be viewed as a blueprint of your life and used to examine what the celestial bodies gifted you with, including your strengths and weaknesses. As it allows insight into your soul's desires, it's often used to increase self-awareness. It helps you realize who you are, your most obvious personality traits, and what you can expect from your future. As mentioned, the prevalent factor to look out for here is your sun sign. However, plenty of other aspects can influence readings in natal astrology.

Horary Astrology

Horary astrology is an ancient divination technique that examines earthly events dating back to 30,000 B.C. It combines the use of the celestial maps created by ancient cultures and modern techniques, very similar to those used in tarot card readings. Despite requiring a look deep into the past, this branch can give you an incredibly accurate insight into future events. Astrologers create a chart specific to the location and the time a question is asked. By interpreting the chart, astrologers can provide "yes" or "no" answers to the question. If they run into a blockage, they can either assume that the answer is not yet ready to be revealed or take a different approach, such as consulting the ancient maps and repeating the question. Because it is so specific, this branch of astrology is practiced by skilled astrologers with a great deal of experience in extracting crucial details and fitting them into simple answers.

Electional Astrology

As its name implies, electional astrology involves choosing the most appropriate time for a particular event based on celestial action. Also called event astrology, this branch is used for planning events as well as predicting when some regular events may happen. It's great for accurately narrowing down the dates for positive occasions. If someone wants to know what astrology says about the best time of the month to go for a job interview, astrology can help them pick the right timing. Other advice that can be requested is when is the best time to meet a new partner, get married, or do anything else people may want to know. A person may choose to avoid an event by planning around retrograde movements of the planets or by looking at the moon. This luminary satellite affects your emotions, which may influence your experience at that particular event.

Mundane Astrology

Mundane astrology looks at the broad picture, examining global events and affairs. It has been widely used for thousands of years. Its origins can be traced back to a time when people were more interested in what the stars held for nations and their rulers. Like horary astrology, its mundane counterpart also takes past events into consideration. It examines patterns and looks at how the future may complete a cycle that began in the past. For example, each time the planets Pluto and Saturn meet, the inhabitants of the Earth experience events of historic proportions. And these events last until the planets start to distance themselves from one another. Mundane astrology can also be viewed as a unique form of birth chart for nations and historical events. Astrologers also use it to look at what happened at a specific time in the past and to predict whether or when it will happen again.

Medical Astrology

This particular branch of astrology links planets and zodiac signs to ailments affecting specific body parts. Planets are associated with organs or organ systems, while zodiac signs influence general areas of the body. This branch is a valuable tool for mapping out personal astrological charts. Astrologers can look at someone's chart and predict ailments the person might be afflicted by in the future. For example, if someone's zodiac sign is Leo, they're most likely to develop chest issues. If, when narrowed down to the planets, it's discovered that the chart shows Mars and Mercury together in Leo, it indicates a possible heart condition in the future. That being said, these predictions are only to be used in conjunction with regular checks with health care providers.

Relationship Astrology

Probably the second most popular branch of astrology, divination related to relationships, is a unique discipline. While it's commonly used for determining compatibility in a romantic relationship, this branch can also be applied to any other type of relationship, from family to friends to work. Synastry is a specific form of relationship divination that directly compares two people's birth charts. The astrologers place one chart over the other and look at any overlapping positions of celestial bodies, zodiac signs, and houses. It helps to see where each person's strengths and abilities to support and relate to each other lie on a day-to-day basis. The composite astrological chart, or relationships chart, looks at the midpoint between the planets for each person, creating a third chart just for their relationship. After placing the two charts on top of each other, the position of the planets and signs are located. Then midpoints between all bodies that do not overlap are also determined. These points are then copied onto a new chart. This helps the astrologer predict the relationship's future and how it will be influenced by celestial actions.

Astrology vs. Astronomy

Since astrology and astronomy are both concerned with planets and other celestial actions, it's not surprising that they have common origins. In fact, back when people didn't make distinctions between science, culture, and religious beliefs, they were considered one and the same. Archeological records show that the terms astrology and astronomy were used interchangeably in ancient times. They represented a unified approach to the study of the sky, and astrological observations were made to improve astronomical predictions. This was the prevailing concept until modern sciences - physics and modern astronomy - showed us the importance of studying how celestial bodies affect each other and not just how they affect life on Earth.

Nowadays, scientists on both sides acknowledge a clear distinction between the two sciences. Modern astronomy is only concerned with the positions, properties, and movements of objects that exist outside of Earth's atmosphere. Astrology, on the other hand, is geared toward discovering how all these objects affect what's happening on Earth. While predictions of celestial phenomena are also employed in astronomy, these are only for scientific purposes.

Using Astrology to Predict the Future

The role of Divinational Astrology lies on several pillars. The most important ones are the position of the celestial bodies and the links between the zodiac signs and their original constellations. Based on this, we know that each moment in time represents a crucial part of an astrological chart. Astrologers can uncover insightful information about someone just by looking at their birth chart. A person's inherent values and qualities determine how they will experience the most significant events in their life. However, astrology can still not predict the future. It will not tell you the exact time of day you can expect to experience something. It only suggests an approximate time based on your actions and personal traits. You can use it to uncover potential opportunities, challenges, conflicts, and life paths. It can help you make meaningful choices about your future. Still, the outcome will depend entirely on your current and future thoughts and actions. If you suddenly change your mind and start thinking and acting differently from how you did at the time of the reading, the outcome may differ drastically. The celestial events can help you predict what the change may be. However, only a very detailed chart can help you reveal how the interactions of the planets and the zodiac signs will influence your life.

The Role of the Zodiac in Astrological Divinations

The term zodiac refers to the cycle completed along the ecliptic. As the sun travels across the sky, it passes through several stellar constellations. These constellations split the celestial ecliptic into twelve equal parts called zodiac houses - elliptical zones linked to the twelve months of the year. The zodiac is the oldest system designed to coordinate the placements and movements of the celestial bodies. The sign rules the month a person was born and their character. It may also indicate they have certain traits to use to their advantage or improve. By consulting your zodiac sign, you access information that helps you make smaller choices.

Ways to Have More Accurate Readings

In their eagerness to learn what the zodiac and the planets may hold for them, many people make mistakes that lead to incorrect readings and misleading information about future events. There are layers to an accurate prediction; the key to getting a clear picture is peeling off all these layers. Below, you'll see what this means and how it helps you do more accurate readings.

Use Full Natal Charts

The best way to access accurate information is to learn everything about the person you're reading for. This means exploring their sun, moon, and rising signs. Remember, the sun signs (the zodiac signs) represent only a small portion of the information pool you can find out about a person. Using only this reduces the chances of fully understanding someone's potential. For better results, create a chart using the person's specific birth location, birth time, and birthdate. This will allow you to create a more comprehensive astrological profile.

Pay Particular Attention to the Ascendant

The ascendant, or rising sign, shows how your personality is likely to be viewed by others. Although how people recognize you is a superficial element in astrology, it still carries weight. How a person interacts with their environment is coded into their core personality, giving you indirect access to it. It's also the fastest way to access crucial information about someone; you don't have to analyze how they think or behave – others have already done this, *even if they do so subconsciously.* Analyzing their opinion will save you considerable time. The ascendant also shows how a person moves through their life. This allows you to predict their future patterns and behaviors more accurately. Once again, it's important to use accurate birth information. The ascendant is the middle of the horizon at the time of birth and sets the basis of the entire chart.

Consult the Moon

Another way to find accurate information about someone's personality is by exploring their feelings. Emotions are ruled by the moon, and learning more about them can reveal someone's true potential. Developing emotions is related to the growth of one's inner world. In fact, how a person develops emotions towards their environment says more about them than how they act and speak. The moon also affects people's ability to nourish their relationships. While this information may contradict what the sun sign says about a person, it's often more accurate.

Improve Compatibility Readings

Their sun sign tells you very little about a person's relationship compatibility. Just as it won't give a clear picture of someone's personality, it won't let you see their value to others. Because relationships are built on common values and the ability to respect other people's values, even if they differ from yours, you'll need to look at the full charts of all people in the relationships you're analyzing. This way, you'll see what works and what doesn't. A person can work on accepting another person's values, but they'll rarely abandon their own. Improving your compatibility readings is also good practice for developing more in-depth personal charts.

Don't Rely Too Much on Retrograde Motion

Despite their challenging nature, retrograde transits are sometimes given too much importance. There is nothing wrong with wanting to avoid their negative impact, but sometimes this isn't possible. In addition, focusing only on what retrograde motions bring could prevent you from predicting small but positive changes. Instead, focus on these helpful signs. By recognizing them, you'll be able to steer the person concerned clear of any mishaps during retrograde. For example, you can plan to avoid anything that involves communication when Mercury is in retrograde. However, instead of trying to avoid making a mistake by evading communication with everyone around you, you can try to make the best of what life offers during the retrograde and focus on expressing your thoughts in other ways.

The Astrological Chart Wheel

General astrology charts can help you interpret several aspects of life, including past patterns, a group's behavior, or a person's nature. This allows you to make more precise predictions about the future related to the subject in question. The astrological chart wheels contain the symbols for the ruling sign and its polarity, the ascendant, the ruling zodiac houses and their opposites, and the placement of the planets. Here is how to decode an astrological chart wheel.

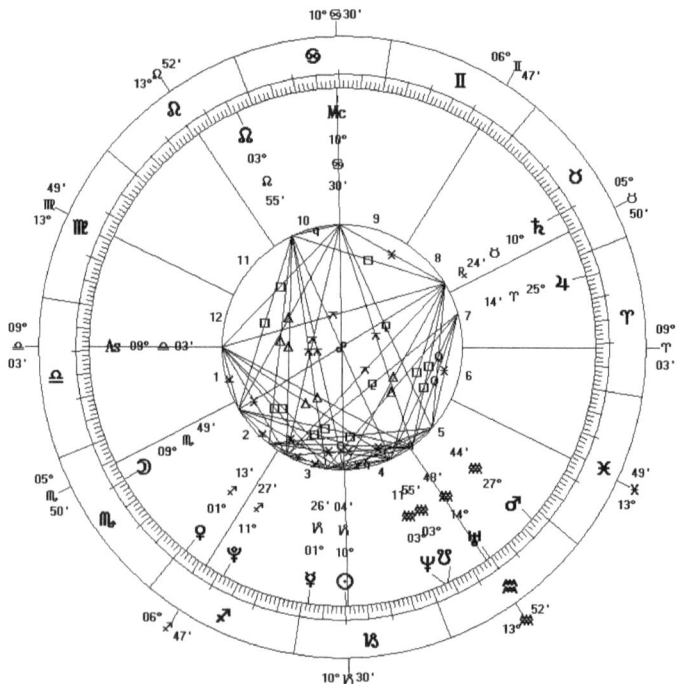

Astrological chart wheel.
*Maksim Attribution-ShareAlike 3.0 Unported (CC BY-SA 3.0) <
https://creativecommons.org/licenses/by-sa/3.0/deed.en>
https://commons.wikimedia.org/wiki/File:Astrological_Chart_-_New_Millennium.JPG*

Locating the Zodiac (Sun) Sign

The 12 zodiac signs, or sun signs, reflect the sun's annual journey across the sky. The symbols and polarities of the signs are as follows:

- ♈ Aries - ♎ Libra
- ♉ Taurus - ♏ Scorpio
- ♊ Gemini - ♐ Sagittarius
- ♋ Cancer - ♑ Capricorn
- ♌ Leo - ♒ Aquarius
- ♍ Virgo - ♓ Pisces

Learning about the Houses

Locations are based on the position and trajectory of the earth as it rotates around its axis over 24 hours. Here are the ruling houses and their opposites, as seen on the chart:

First I - Seventh VII
Second II - Eighth VIII
Third III - Ninth IX
Fourth IV - Tenth X
Fifth V - Eleventh XI
Sixth VI - Twelfth XII

Understanding the Planets

Here are planets affecting a chart. They are divided into personal planets (like the sun, the moon, and Mercury) and outer planets (all the other planets).

☉ **Sun** - Responsible for self-esteem, confidence, self-image, and sense of identity

☾ **Moon** - Shapes the values, emotions, and intuition and provides an emotional compass

☿ **Mercury** - Rules over communication, the ability to research and collect information

♀ **Venus** - Influences art, relationships, passion, pleasure, money, and beauty

♂ **Mars** - Prompts action and increases tension, expression, courage, and sexuality

♃ **Jupiter** - Responsible for luck, abundance, and prosperity

♄ **Saturn** - Creates boundaries, rules, limitations, and discipline

♅ **Uranus** - Allows breakthrough, rebellion, and sudden changes and events

♆ **Neptune** - Involved in spirituality, intuition, and developing compassion and ideals

♇ **Pluto** - The Planet of rebirth, death, transformation, and power

Aspects

The aspects of the chart determine how the different positions are related to each other. Here are the symbols of the common ones:

☌ Conjunction

⚼ Sesquiquadrate

⚺ Semi-sextile

⚻ Quincunx

✶ Sextile

☍ Opposition

□ Square

△ Trine

∠ Semi-Square

Other Points and Symbols

Another pertinent symbol in astrological symbols is the ascendant, which is the sign ascending on the eastern horizon at the time of a person's birth. Apart from this, other points may be presented, depending on how detailed you want to make the chart. Here are some other symbols you might encounter:

☊ North Node
Mc Midheaven
☋ South Node
Vx Vertex
R Retrograde
⚷ Chiron
⚳ Ceres
⚵ Juno
⚴ Pallas
⚶ Vesta

Chapter 3: Decoding Your Birth Chart

Your natal chart can give you insight into your life's purpose. This map shows the available paths, areas of abundance, and possible problems you may face. Since it is a map, learning to read it can give you all the guidance you need about where to go and what you need to do to get there. Your birth chart is your go-to guide for self-growth and development. It highlights all the qualities you need to work on and the areas you need to pay attention to throughout your life's journey. A natal chart outlines your life's purpose and how you should go about it.

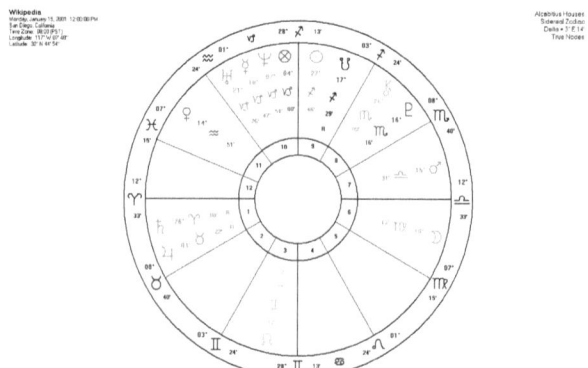

Your natal chart can give you insight into your life's purpose. Source: John Charles Webb at English Wikipedia, https://commons.wikimedia.org/wiki/File:Wikipedia_Sidereal_Birth_Chart.gif

What Is a Birth Chart?

You can think of your birth chart as a 2D map or screenshot of what the sky looked like at the exact time and place of your birth. If you can't read a birth chart or at least gain a basic understanding of it, it will probably look like a confusing collection of lines and symbols. This is why learning to decode your birth chart can be a bit intimidating at first. Natal charts speak their own language, and it takes a decent amount of time, energy, and dedication for them to start making sense to you. However, putting in the effort is well worth it. You can make a free birth chart online using your date of birth, time, and place of birth.

The Time of Birth

The planets and the stars are constantly on the move. Everything in the sky is always in motion. Whether we realize it or not, the sky looks different each minute. If you are plotting your birth chart, it is essential to know the exact time of your birth. You might not know the exact time of your birth, but there is sure to be a family member who will know.

Don't be discouraged if no one seems to know your birth time. You can use an estimate. Look up the exact time of sunrise on your date of birth for a sunrise chart. You can also use a noon chart - just put in 12 p.m. You can always seek the help of an expert astrologer too! They can give you an in-depth reading of natal chart rectification. This means that they'll ask you specific questions about your life that can help them uncover your birth time.

The Location of Birth

At this moment, the sky looks different everywhere in the world. The sun sets and rises at different times, and the constellations appear and disappear in different places depending on where you are in the world. This is why birth location is another crucial piece of the puzzle. The location of birth accurately determines what the sky looked like at the time of your birth, and it says a lot about your character and personality.

It Is Where You, Time, Earth, Space, and the Sky Meet

Most online charts generate a wheel or circular birth chart. However, some traditions may depict it in the shape of a square (or other shapes).

One thing you need to know about reading a birth chart is that you shouldn't read it by looking at it from above. Birth charts are read as if you are right in the center of a 3D construction. This can be confusing because the directions are then flipped. If you're using a regular compass, West would be to the left and East to the right. North is up, and South is down. However, when reading a natal chart, your East is West, and your North is South.

Why Are Birth Charts Significant to Divination Practices?

What benefit would be gained if you learned that Mercury makes a trine to your Neptune or that Uranus is square to your ascendant? Mastering the art of decoding birth charts can't be done overnight. So, is it really worth the hassle?

If you're already active in divination, then you're probably already aware of just how comprehensive the study of Astrology is. It touches upon every aspect of your life, allowing you to discover who you really are. It teaches you all about your core needs, desires, and motives in life and provides insight into who you are meant to be.

Your birth chart uses the language of stars and the positions of the planet to dive into your psyche. It's a way to find out what you're capable of and how to take a step closer to unlocking your full potential. Analyzing your natal chart helps you learn about your talents. We're not only referring to musical, athletic, or artistic endeavors, but we're also talking about one's soft skills. Astrological charts also identify people's weaknesses. Whether you have trouble controlling your anger or go into a self-destructive mode when you're stressed, decoding your birth chart can help you learn more about yourself and make the changes necessary to heal or control these weaknesses and capitalize on your strengths.

If you learn how to use it correctly, you'll get to know yourself so much better in every area of your life, and you'll soon be able to share your knowledge with others. With practice, you'll be able to do readings for your close friends and family, which will also teach you a lot about them. You'll begin to understand the things that make your loved ones feel uneasy. You'll know to look at the moon for answers when you want to know what makes someone feel safe and secure. You'll immediately navigate to your Venus if you wish to explore your love language.

You can improve your relationship with anyone by studying their natal chart. It helps you understand how they approach their relationships, what they look for in friends and partners, what they respond to, and how they express their love. Even if you're both completely different or if you have disagreements, learning about that person can help you become more empathetic and compassionate toward them. When you find out what motives and desires they're driven by and what their core needs are, you'll come to know why that person behaves, feels, or thinks the way they do. This also applies to your relationship with yourself. Instead of criticizing your actions, you'll grow to appreciate yourself and surround yourself with people who appreciate you.

Birth charts can be an incredible tool whenever you need to patch things up after getting into a conflict with someone. For instance, if you tell your friend off for being extra moody, you'll become more understanding once you find out they're a Scorpio moon. Scorpio moons are usually very sensitive to the vibes around them. They can easily take in both bad and good energy, which makes it hard for them to control their moods. A Scorpio moon could be having the best day ever before it all turns upside down when they interact with a friend who feels down.

Studying someone's birth chart reveals their natural patterns. You could also compare both of your charts to find out if your energy matches theirs. Learning that each of you expresses yourself and approaches conflict differently will help you to put things into perspective. It reminds you to take a moment and pause whenever you feel angry or confused about any aspects of your relationship. Birth charts are significant to divination practices because they dive deeply into several aspects of one's personality and being.

How to Decode Your Birth Chart
Before We Start

What Is the Ascendant?

Your ascendant or rising sign can be found in the Eastern hemisphere on the left side of the chart. It's called the rising sign because this is where the Sun rises. The degree of your ascending is that of the rising at the time and location of your birth. This is the point that most deeply and closely represents you.

What Is the Midheaven - MC?

The Midheaven or MC is basically the Southern hemisphere on your birth chart. It is the high noon and is when the Sun reaches its highest point in the sky. It is representative of your general image and professional success.

What Is the Descendant - DC?

The descendant is where the sun sets in the Western hemisphere. It is representative of your relationships and interactions.

What Is the Imum Coeli - IC?

The Imum Coeli is the midnight of your birth chart and can be found in the Northern hemisphere. It has everything to do with your inner life.

Birth Chart Components

The planets, the aspects of the planets, the signs, and the houses are the four core components of the birth chart.

Planets

Our motives and drive are represented by the planets. For instance, the drive to love and build intimate connections with people is ruled by Venus, while Mars represents the drive to win and succeed. Traditionally, our main focus in the birth chart is the planets we can see from Earth with just our naked eye. Mars, Venus, Saturn, and Jupiter can all be seen by the naked eye, along with, of course, the sun and the moon. Now, with the help of modern technology, we can add Pluto, Neptune, Uranus, and minor celestial bodies. The following are the roles of the planets:

Sun - Represents your identity and how you stand out.

Moon - Rules our emotions and bodies.

Mercury - Associated with how we communicate and where we do it.

Venus- Deals with how we connect with others and where we do it.

Mars - Related to how we take action and in which areas of life.

Jupiter - Linked to how you create abundance and where you'll find/create it in life.

Saturn - Represents our boundaries, how we create them, and where we do them.

Uranus - Related to how we innovate and think out of the box.

Neptune - Associated with how we use our imagination and the areas where we use it the most.

Pluto - Rules over how we possess our secret power and where we hold it.

Aspects

Aspects are representative of the relationships between the planets. They're just like us. Some planets get along, while others don't work well together. Some have neutral relationships, and a few don't deal with others at all. If you work toward self-awareness and put in the effort necessary, you can get all the planets to make peace with each other. Instead of a challenging birth chart, you can end up with one that is supportive and helpful. The following are the traditional aspects:

Gifts

Sextiles: planets that are 60 degrees or 2 signs apart are called sextiles. For instance, one planet can be in a fire/earth sign while another lies in an air/water sign, respectively. Since these planets work well together, sextiles are considered gifts. However, they are a little less intense than trines.

Trines: Planets that are 1/3 of a full revolution apart – planets that are 120 degrees or 4 signs apart. These planets co-exist harmoniously and communicate seamlessly. They bring protection, comfort, and blessings into your life.

Challenges

Squares: planets that are 3 signs apart are called squares. For instance, a planet that falls in Scorpio and another in Leo would make a square. These planets are a bit harsh, and they urge you to take action. They cause points of friction.

Oppositions: planets that are 6 signs apart are called oppositions. As the name describes, these planets lie in signs that are opposite to each other, which is why they're the most challenging. Whenever we feel overwhelmed, we need to find a way to create a balance between those opposing forces. We are encouraged to take a moment to think about what we offer to the world and what we must take from it.

Mergers

Conjunctions: planets that lie in the same sign as another are known as conjunctions. The closer those two planets are, the more their energies will amalgamate, generating unique traits and properties.

Signs

The signs represent how the planets express themselves. They guide the planet's mood, manner, and style of expression. The following are the 12 signs and each of their styles:

Aries: Action-driven, self-determining, and independent

Taurus: Grounded, sensible, and stable

Gemini: Conversational, intrigued, and curious

Cancer: Emotive, sensitive, and caring

Leo: Entertaining, charming, and expressive

Virgo: Analytical, observant, and perfecting

Libra: Justice-seeking, adaptable, and accommodating

Scorpio: Pervasive, perceptive, and mysterious

Sagittarius: Positive, cheerful, and hopeful

Capricorn: Self-controlled and disciplined

Aquarius: Intellectual, decisive, and definitive.

Pisces: Creative, innovative, and sensitive.

The signs serve as the planets' residences. According to traditional astrologers, the 7 planets we can see with the naked eye build unique relationships with the signs. Some planets thrive in some signs and, conversely, feel extremely uneasy in others. The signs also play another role. They divide the natal chart's 360 degrees into twelve 30-degree parts. Since the chart symbolically represents the sky to help us grasp a better understanding of it, the zodiac signs are also a symbolic reference to the constellations that are traversed by the sun from our perspective on Earth. This path is called the ecliptic.

Since these are all symbolic depictions, they're not all accurate. For instance, the constellations don't really make up twelve parts of 30 equal degrees. Take Virgo and Libra as an example: the former is twice the size of the latter. However, the birth chart serves the purpose of any other map. It aims to make things easier for us to grasp.

Houses

There are 12 houses, each representing a different area of life. The following are the different houses and the different areas that they govern:

The 1st House: Vitality, life, image and appearance, body, and self.

The 2nd House: Assets, belonging, income, resources, and living

The 3rd House: Communication, interactions, routine, daily life, relatives, and siblings

The 4th House: Parents, structure, essence, and home.

The 5th House: Creative endeavors, pleasure, intimacy, sex, and children

The 6th House: Health and professional life

The 7th House: Romantic partners, partnerships, and other commitments

The 8th House: Mental health, the resources of others, and death

The 9th House: Education, travel, spirituality, philosophy, religion, publishing, and astrology

The 10th House: Public image or role and career

The 11th House: Community, society, friends, good fortune, and sponsors

The 12th House: Sorrow, sadness, loss, secrets, mysteries, and hidden aspects of life

Even though the solar system determines which planets lie in the different signs, the "houses" depend on the moment and place of your birth. You may still be confused between the planets and the houses. Here's a trick to help you distinguish between both:

The moon is the fastest-moving celestial body. It takes around 2 or 3 days to pass through a sign. However, it only takes 24 hours to pass through all the houses in the natal chart. This is the same for all planets, as well. For instance, it would take Pluto anywhere between 12 to 32 years to make it through just one sign, while it takes only 24 hours to traverse all the houses.

How to Use a Birth Chart

Find an online tool to generate your birth chart.

You may be asked to enter your name, date of birth, time of birth, and location of birth.

Don't overwhelm yourself by trying to make sense of the entire chart at once. Start by observing the big three: your Sun, Moon, and rising signs. These will help you learn a lot about who you are.

For the coming three months, select one sign to focus on for an entire month. Meditate on the planet or the sign's aspects and think about how you relate to it, how you embody its energy, and how you wish to do it.

Keep a special birth chart notebook where you can journal all about your revelations and mental notes.

Even though you now have a better idea of what all the components of the natal chart mean and the roles that they serve, putting the pieces together can still be a challenge. It will take time until you are able to give an accurate birth chart reading. However, the learning journey is incredibly interesting and satisfying. Once you master the art of birth chart reading, you'll discover that you've unlocked a new language of expression; the language of the stars. You'll understand things about yourself that you've struggled to make sense of for years. Your life's purpose will suddenly become clear right before your eyes. The paths you are destined to take, the lessons that you need to learn, and the ways in which you need to grow and develop will all make more sense to you.

Chapter 4: Numerology

Numerology takes the numbers that are apparent in the world around us and applies them to our path through life. Think of numerology as a universal language but instead of using words, it uses numbers. In numerology, numbers have an energetic influence on people's lives, just like astrology and how the planets' alignments can impact your personality. Numerology can help you learn more about yourself, the world around you, and the people in your life. It is based on the theory that if you break down the universe's system, you will be left with the basic elements. These basic elements are *numbers*.

1.	2.	3.	4.	5.	6.	7.	8.	9.	10.	20.	30.	40.
A.	B.	C.	D.	E.	F.	G.	H.	I.	K.	L.	M.	N.
50.	60.	70.	80.	90.	100.	200.	300.	400.	500.	600.	700.	800.
O.	P.	Q.	R.	S.	T.	V.	X.	Y.	Z.	I.	V.	HI.
900.												
HV.												

Agrippan method of numerology.
https://commons.wikimedia.org/wiki/File:Agrippan_numerology_table.jpg

    This may sound a little complicated for some people, as many usually associate numbers with mathematics. Most people take numbers for granted. Like the air you breathe, you don't think twice about its importance or what it means. You just inhale and exhale. However, numbers are much more powerful than you can imagine.

On a cosmic level, numbers are considered symbols with strong, energetic vibrations that impact each and every person in the world. That said, not all numbers carry the same vibration; each number is unique, and so is its impact on individuals. Each number's vibration has its own properties, giving you an idea of your main characteristics and compatibility with potential romantic partners. Numerology can also help you discover your lucky day and lucky number. In numerology, everything happens for a reason, and this reason is numbers.

Everything related to you is made of numbers. Take a look at your birthday. It is made of numbers. Although your name is made of letters, these letters correspond with certain numbers which define who you are and impact your life's path. The same applies to your phone number, address, salary, etc. There are numbers everywhere around you and deep inside of you, so it makes sense that numerology will affect your life in different ways.

Numbers can affect your destiny as well as every part of your life, including your personality and certain life events. Numerology and astrology are deeply linked – numerology also deals with all the large heavenly bodies (the major planets) in our solar system (including Neptune, the sun, and the moon). There are usually two planets that govern your birth date, one primary and one secondary. Each person gives out vibrations of the planet and numbers associated with their name and birth.

Learning numerology can be overwhelming since there are various ways to navigate through it. However, having a background in astrology will help get you started, as it means that you are already familiar with numerology. In fact, you'll find more than a few similarities between the two subjects. Although Astrology and Numerology can help you gain more insight into yourself and the world around you, each uses its own method. Numerology works by calculating the numbers that make up your date of birth and the numbers associated with every letter in your name.

The History of Numerology

Numerology is an ancient study, and its origin is quite a mystery. Similar to many ancient philosophies, no one knows exactly where numerology originated. Some people believe that the Babylonians and ancient Egyptians first used numerology. There is evidence that shows that Japan, China, Rome, and Greece also used numerology during ancient times. However, most people in modern times believe that the Greek philosopher and mathematician Pythagoras was the one whose theories most influenced the study of numerology. For this reason, he is often referred to as the father of numerology. No one knows for a fact whether it was Pythagoras or someone else who invented numerology. Just like the origin of numerology, Pythagoras's life remains a mystery, but his passion for numbers is a well-known fact. His mathematical theories have changed the way people in the modern world regard and treat numbers.

According to Pythagoras, numbers are extremely powerful in that they govern the world, and everything in life can be translated into single digits. Each letter is assigned a number which is called the Pythagorean Number System. This system is one of the fundamental bases of modern numerology. People use this system in different areas of their lives; however, in modern times, people use it the same way they use astrology to help them better understand themselves and to predict the future.

During ancient times, people believed that there were real powers behind each number. They also believed that the essence of the divine could be found in numbers, which could help them learn about God and themselves. This was when the oldest known form of numerology, the Chaldean System of Numerology, was used. In the Middle East and Asia, the study of numerology focused on the numbers in religious texts and their impact on people's lives.

Numerology and Astrology Combined

Numerology and astrology use different methods, yet both can help you better understand yourself and the world around you. Astrology studies the influence of the planets' positions on people's lives to help them find their true purpose in life. It also employs the power of the horoscope to predict the future. On the other hand, numerology uses various numbers associated with your life which can help you uncover information that will guide you in life. As mentioned, numerology uses your birthdate and name to create a chart, and astrology and numerology share the same foundation, which is mathematics. You need numbers to calculate the positions of the stars, their angles, and degrees at the time of your birth. Most people see astrology as a tool that helps you understand your personality and predict the future. However, you can't get there without mathematics. Since mathematics is all about numbers, this means that astrology and numerology can be interconnected and create a study that is referred to as astro-numerology.

You can combine the two to reveal your unique personality traits and pave your path through life. In fact, Pythagoras combined the two by associating stars with numbers. He later discovered that the two were very much connected since the planets, stars, and numbers were all intertwined. When combined together, both subjects can be much more powerful. That said, you don't have to be an expert in astrology to perform a numerology reading. All you need is to have an idea of every planet and its influence. Each number from 0 to 9 is ruled by a planet, the moon, or the sun.

Zero is ruled by Pluto

One is ruled by Sun

Two is ruled by Moon

Three is ruled by Jupiter

Four is ruled by Earth

Five is ruled by Mercury

Six is ruled by Venus

Seven is ruled by Neptune

Eight is ruled by Saturn

Nine is ruled by Mars

The moon, sun, and planets are connected with the energy and vibrations of each number. Using the combination of the two arts, one can get a deeper and more insightful look into their personality and life path.

The Various Origins of Numerological Systems

Throughout history, there is clear evidence that Many cultures used numerology. There were two methods that were commonly used during these times: Kabbalah Numerology and Chaldean Numerology. Later Pythagoras developed his own method, which is called Pythagorean Numerology, and people still use it to this day. Understanding the different methods of numerology will help you with your reading. Choose the method that you can understand and feel connected with. It is recommended that you stick to one method to avoid confusing yourself, especially if you are a beginner.

The Pythagorean Numerology System

Pythagoras was a Greek Philosopher and Mathematician who is often regarded as one of the fathers of modern mathematics. He developed his famous theorem when he was studying musical instruments and discovered that they vibrated at different levels – each of which he could attribute to a different number. The theorem he developed from studying music changed geometry as we know it and, importantly, showed a connection between the physical world and numbers. We can use Pythagoras's theorem to gain deeper insights into our lives and futures.

With the neurology system from Pythagoras, we can connect letters to numbers and use the letters revealed from dates of birth and names at birth to generate a series of numbers that can reveal our fate. Each person's name has its own number, and if a person decides to change their name, they will get assigned a new number. A person's name impacts their nature and personality; if they change their name, their nature and personality will most likely change as well. The idea of changing a name may be confusing in modern times. However, this is a tactic that Pythagoras used to change a person's destiny.

In the Pythagorean Numerology System, the basic vibrations begin from the numbers one to nine. While the master vibrations are numbers 11, 22, and 33. Master numbers should not be taken down to individual digits.

This method works with six types of numerology numbers:

Birthday number

Personality number

Power number

Attitude number

Soul number

Life path number

The Chaldean Numerology System

This system shares the most similarities with astrology. In fact, the Chaldean Numerology system and Western astrology both originated in Mesopotamia. The Chaldeans were an ancient group of people from Babylonia. They were intelligent people and knew that thoughts and words could influence the energy around people. The Chaldean Numerology system does not differ very much from the Kabbalah system of numbers or the Vedic system. You'll find a range of number systems across the globe that are all very similar in nature. The Pythagorean Numerology System differs a little and uses all the numbers from 1 to 9, while the other systems regard 9 as a sacred number and do not include it. Each letter has its own unique vibration, and each number has its own energetic quality, so letters are assigned to any number from one to eight.

The Chaldean system also has master numbers: 11, 22, and 33, and as with the Pythagorean system, they should not be reduced to a single digit. When the two systems are looked at, the Chaldean is the older of the two, suggesting that the Pythagorean system borrowed from it. But while they are similar in essence, they differ in how they calculate a fate or future, so they should not be used interchangeably. Individual digits are used to discover personality and traits. On the other hand, double-digit numbers can help uncover a person's inner personality, the deeply private one. When using the numbers to calculate from a name, the Chaldean system derives social status from the first name, the energy of the soul from the second, and self-image from a surname.

The Kabbalistic Numerology System

A system of Hebrew letters used to interpret people's names – it contained 22 vibrations. The Greeks and the Romans later adapted it into their own alphabets. Later in the 13th century, an interesting discovery was made as more people began using the Kabbalah system. They believed that God wrote the Old Testament using a secret code, and numerology was their best option to interpret the code and decipher its secrets. To a great extent, the twenty-two vibrations in this system also helped interpret the twenty-two tarot trump cards.

This method stands out from other Numerology systems as it only uses a person's name, but it doesn't use their birthdate, which makes it different from astrology which is based mainly on the person's birthdate. Numbers don't share the same values in different numerological systems. Even if the systems share similar methods, this doesn't guarantee that the value of numbers will be the same or give you the same results. It may not be easy for beginners to fully comprehend the Kabbalah system. This doesn't mean that it's impossible; it will just take you a bit longer. The system of Kabbalah has a central theme of balance and harmony, and there are between 1-400 integration paths depending on the unique vibration.

The Tamil Numerology System

The Tamil Numerology system is one of the most ancient numerological systems. This system originated in India, which is why it is also referred to as the Indian Numerology System. The Tamil system can give you a better insight into yourself so you can uncover your potential and learn about your abilities. You'll be able to look at the world in a different way and better see the path laid out before you. This system can deepen your connection with the world around you, especially during harsh times. It uses the planets' energies and their positions to help you learn about your personality and temperament.

The Tamil Numerology system focuses on the Name Number, Destiny Number, and Psychic Number in a person's calculations.

The Chinese Numerology System

As with most number systems, there are meanings associated with different numbers. And, within that, some numbers are luckier than others. In Chinese numerology, pairs of numbers are very important, and this theme of twos makes even numbers luckier than odd ones. Numerology also connects to acupuncture, and the body is divided by numbers, helping practitioners find points on the body depending on the number.

Angel Numbers and Angelic Numerology

This "angel/angelic" system is newer – especially when compared to some of the other numerology systems, and it does not have ties to the original systems of numerology, though it is influenced by them. It is believed that numbers have their own vibrations that can influence people. When taken further, the vibrations can be seen as created by design, and God created Angel Numbers as a way for heavenly beings to communicate. The most powerful numbers are the ones that repeat (have you ever wondered why we make a wish at 11:11? It can be traced to Angel Numbers). The same power comes in other repeated numbers and not just 11:11. Reading these numbers can help connect you with angels and reveal the divine powers and magic in your life.

How Numerology Can Deepen Your Understanding of Yourself

Consider numerology as a cheat sheet to help you figure out your true potential and uncover your inner self. Interestingly, the two things that are out of your control - your name and your birthdate - can influence who you are and how you live your life. Once you crack it using numerology, they contain a code that will help you discover your life's secrets. You have probably heard others saying that life would be much easier if people came with a manual. Well, you can consider numerology as a manual or guide that can help you learn about your various personality traits and better understand those around you as well.

Numerology has quite a number of uses. It can guide you toward finding meaning in your life and put you in the right direction. You can also use it to give you an idea of the kind of energy that will impact your life in the future. For instance, you can use numerology when naming your child since a person's name is extremely powerful and can impact their potential and personality.

You are often told who you should be or how you should act, either by your family, school, friends, or social media. Numerology is what can give you a great insight into your true potential and who you really are, away from all the outside influences and loud noise. Use this information to better understand yourself and improve your life. Similar to having a zodiac sign in astrology, in numerology, each person has a Life Path Number which can help them learn about who they really are and challenge them to answer life's most complicated questions.

There is a reason people have been fascinated with astrology for so long, as it can help them answer life's most difficult questions, such as who am I? Why am I here? Numerology can also help you solve the biggest mystery of all, yourself, and unlock your true potential. Using both subjects together can give you the answers you are hoping for.

Chapter 5: Your Life Path Number

Do you have a lucky number that you keep seeing in the strangest places? Each person has a life path number that is like their shadow. It is always with you wherever you go. You can see this number reflected in the things that inspire you; it gives you a sense of purpose and helps you to see your true life objectives. Your life path number, also called the destiny number in Chaldean numerology, is quite similar to your zodiac sign. You need to discover it to take advantage of all the information it offers. Many people often feel lost and struggle to find their place in the world, but armed with the information from your life path number, you'll find a sense of direction and grounding whenever life discourages or distracts you.

This number represents your core essence, which makes finding out what it is even more of a necessity. The art of numerology believes each person has a numerological destiny, and the key is your life path number. Aligning yourself to it will help you reach your numerological destiny and give you a better understanding of your life.

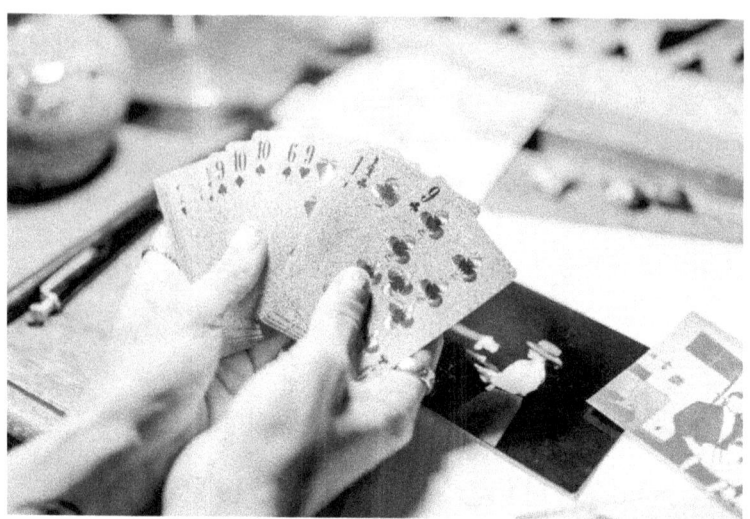
Each person has a life path number that is like their shadow.
https://www.pexels.com/photo/wood-nature-man-people-6806434/

Your life path number is any number from one to nine or 11, 22, or 33, which are referred to as master numbers. Just like zodiac signs, each of the basic and master numbers represents certain characteristics, weaknesses, and strengths. There is more than one type of zodiac sign - your sun sign and your moon sign - but the sun sign is usually the most significant. The same applies to numerology, and although there is more than one number in the numerological chart, no number is more significant than your life path number.

Your life path number helps you find your spiritual calling and uncover your deepest desire. For instance, if your life path number is two, this means that your spiritual purpose in life is to bring others peace. This prominent number can help you find the right career based on your skills, abilities, and personality. For instance, if your life path number is one or eight, you'll excel in jobs requiring leadership. However, if your life path number is two or three, you would be better suited for a career in the arts.

The Meaning behind Each Life Path Number

There is a special meaning behind each of the basic and master numbers. Before you learn how to calculate your life path number, you should first learn about the main characteristics behind each one to better understand your personality.

Life Path One

Life path number one individuals are known for their leadership qualities and independent personality. These natural-born leaders have the strength and determination to change the world around them. They have the qualities that are necessary to be great leaders, like originality, confidence, and independence. These individuals know how to achieve their goals and have the creativity to help them achieve anything they set their minds to. These people are destined to lead independent lives and learn how to stand on their own two feet without anyone else's help. You'll never find a life path one individual paying attention to other people's opinions or judgments regarding their lives. They are the ones who take the road less traveled. They lead an authentic and passionate life by being unapologetically themselves.

Their ambition is obvious in the way they go after their goals. They are willing to do whatever is necessary and have a clear vision and strategy that will get them there. They are risk-takers who don't hesitate when it comes to trying out new methods, even if they are dangerous or risky. They are not the type to walk away from something just because someone discourages them or tells them it isn't a good idea. They are brave enough to trust their gut and do things in their own way. In fact, this is usually how they achieve their goals. When this life path isn't in alignment, these individuals can be controlling, selfish, and extremely pragmatic. They can also struggle with overthinking and low self-confidence.

Life Path Two

These individuals are called peacemakers because of their understanding, gentle nature, and ability to mediate to restore peace. These peace-loving souls create balance and harmony wherever they go. It is essential for them to feel needed and loved by everyone they meet. However, love without respect is meaningless to them. In fact, they want to feel valued and appreciated for what they do. These people are great team players because they enjoy brainstorming and sharing ideas with other like-minded individuals. Whether it's their family or friend group, life path two individuals often act like a mother to all the people in their lives. They take care of their needs and provide for them.

If you have a life path two in your life, never lie or betray people with this life path because once you do, you'll lose their trust forever. These individuals are extremely devoted to their loved ones and emotionally sensitive. However, there are moments when they find their emotions overwhelming. They also often struggle with opening up and trusting others.

Life Path Three

It is very easy to feel drawn to the life path of three individuals. They have magnetic personalities, great communication skills, and are very charismatic. They find it easy to communicate with others and don't shy away from self-expression. They are emotionally sensitive, which is evident from how they treat everyone. Thanks to their extroverted nature, these individuals can easily make friends and are often the life and soul of the party. You'll find that they can achieve anything they set their minds to because of their confidence in their abilities and people skills. Although they are likable, and everyone seems to gravitate toward them, they sometimes find it hard to relate to other people's struggles. They don't like to show vulnerability or ask for help. However, maybe being vulnerable is what they need in order to relate to and connect with others.

Life Path Four

These individuals thrive in a stable environment. Hard-working and logical, they will do whatever it takes to achieve their goals. However, if they don't love what they do, they may struggle and fail. Because they are logical and dependable, their friends, family, and co-workers often come to them when in need because they know they can depend on them for support. They are realistic individuals who are focused on achieving their goals; they don't let anything or anyone distract them. They can be very stubborn and inflexible when it comes to their beliefs. It is impossible to change their minds.

Life Path Five

Life path five people are free-spirited individuals who are full of energy. They want to live an adventurous and free life without fear. In fact, freedom is their main purpose in life, so they often struggle with being committed to a person or place. They live life to the fullest and enjoy everything life has to offer; the good, the bad, and the ugly. This may make them seem indulgent and unpredictable, as they will do anything for the sake of a good adventure. Unlike life path four, these individuals can't stand routine or stagnation and thrive in change. They aren't the ones to stay in a job they hate and don't mind changing jobs until they find something they can be passionate about. Because of their adaptability, they can easily integrate into a new workplace.

These people need to be on the move, or they will feel stuck and suffocated. However, this can affect their relationships and make them seem selfish and irresponsible. Having an adventurous spirit can be an admirable quality as long as they remember that they have people in their lives that they can't neglect or leave behind.

Life Path Six

The aim of these people is to live selfless lives and to care for and nurture the people in their lives. They also have strong leadership skills, which is why they prefer to have their own businesses so they can be their own boss. They often act as counselors to their family and friends and manage to keep the peace. Life path six stands out as the least biased out of all the other life paths, thanks to its open-minded nature. They are fair individuals who just want to help others. These individuals can't tolerate injustice and are brave enough to speak up against it. As caring as these people are to those around them, it will benefit them to remember to look out for and care for themselves as well.

Life Path Seven

Just like cats, life path seven individuals are very curious and will do anything to satisfy their thirst for knowledge. They also want to lead a spiritual life focusing on their emotional side and intuition. Their heads are often in the clouds and tend to get caught up in what-if scenarios. They prefer to live with these scenarios in their heads than go out there and experience them in the real world. They spend their lives in search of the truth and are admired for their logical and creative nature.

These individuals are very sensitive and emotional. However, in a harsh world where sensitivity can be perceived as a weakness, they may feel like they don't belong and that they are different from everyone around them. This leads to struggles when connecting with strangers, often accompanied by overthinking situations and projections. However, they can control their overthinking by digging deep and finding ways to trust themselves and their abilities. Being different is nothing to be ashamed of. On the contrary, it should be celebrated.

Life path seven individuals need to give themselves a chance to discover who they are. When they connect with themselves, they can connect with others and develop real and deep relationships.

Life Path Eight

Life path eight individuals want to leave their mark on the world. Their motto is to "Go big or go home," and they have it in them to do this and anything else they set their mind to. Their goal is to succeed, and more times than not, it can be the only thing they focus on, which is why they tend to gravitate toward areas like finance or business. These individuals thrive when working in a team because they believe that working with others can help them achieve the success they very much desire. But their need to control everything can cause them to have trouble with anxiety. They need to relax, let go and believe that some things are out of their control.

Life Path Nine

Life path nine is the last of the basic numbers. Wise, creative, compassionate, generous, and humanitarian, they are the first to help those in their social circle and their community. These individuals believe they can make the world a better place through humanitarian work and connecting with other people. In fact, they inspire and motivate others to go out and help those in need and the less fortunate. Being selfless is an admirable quality. However, their selfless nature makes them so focused on others that they neglect their own needs. They may have trouble finding love because they are often afraid of showing how weak they think they are and letting others in. They shouldn't shy away from expressing their feelings and should remember to ask for help whenever they need it.

Life Path Eleven

The first of the master numbers, life path eleven individuals possess psychic abilities and strong vibrations. The goal is to find the ultimate path in life along with an equilibrium of the spirit and higher knowledge. These people are kind, helpful, and patient and use their special skills to inspire and help others. Just as they care about achieving a spiritual balance, they often inspire others to also go on a spiritual journey to discover themselves. Like everyone else, these individuals may experience unfortunate situations. However, they don't let anything bring them down and will often come out stronger than ever. This is why many people find them inspiring, and they also touch others with their kindness and big heart.

Life Path Twenty-Two

You know the saying that instead of giving a man a fish and feeding him for a day, teach him how to fish, and you'll feed him for the rest of his life? Well, life path 22 individuals believe in this saying wholeheartedly. They want to live a life where they can help others and make a difference in the world. However, they believe that the best way to make a difference in someone's life is by giving them the tools to succeed. People like this are persistent, happy, reliable, and full of wisdom. They are very creative and believe they can achieve anything they set their mind to if they harness their abilities.

Life Path Thirty-Three

Similar to other life path numbers on the list, these people live their lives to help others by using their healing and nurturing abilities. They want to make a difference in the world around them and be known as the loving and compassionate individuals they truly are. They are selfless, and there is nothing that they won't do to help anyone in need. At times, they can be so focused on helping others that they forget to be compassionate and end up being self-righteous and critical. If they manage to let go of their judgmental side, these individuals can be a force of healing in the world.

Calculating Your Life Path Number

You have gained insight into the numbers and what they mean. You can use this knowledge to easily find your life path number. All you need to do is keep adding all the digits in your birthdate until you get one single number. The following example will make things clearer and easier to understand.

For instance, your birth date is March 6th, 1992, 3/6/1992

Add the digits in the year to reduce it to one single digit. 1+9+9+2= 21. You are left with a double-digit, which means you must simplify them.

Take your two numbers and add them: 2+1=3.

Now, add the numbers that represent the month (3) and day (6): 3+6+3= 12.

You do not yet have a single-digit number, so you need to add the two digits together in the number 12: 1+2=3. Now, you have your number.

Always take the digits of any double-digit number and add them together before adding any other numbers to them. If the day or month are double-digit numbers, add them together before adding them to other numbers. However, if the results are 11, 22, or 33, don't add these numbers as they are master numbers and have their meaning in numerology.

Enneagram Number

The Enneagram number is yet another tool to help you better understand yourself. An enneagram is a psychometric assessment of your personality. It shares similarities with numerology since both can help you learn about your characteristics and personality traits from your birth date. However, the enneagram also focuses on how you behave or act in various situations throughout your life. For example, your behavior when you are stressed. There are nine personality types in the enneagram system, and like numerology, each type is associated with a number. The best method to find your enneagram number is by taking an online test. A simple online search will take you to various websites, many of which are free, where you can take the test and learn not only about your personality but your motivations to act a certain way.

If there is a person that you should know more than anyone else, it's yourself. However, most people struggle to understand themselves and find their true purpose in life. Discovering your life path number will help you discover your purpose. Calculating this number is very easy. Just keep one thing in mind. The number you calculate should be a single digit. If you have double-digit numbers in your date of birth (for example, the month is November (11)), you need to add them together before adding them to any other numbers. The only exception to this rule is when you are adding your final life path number and you get a double-digit number with the same number (like 22). These powerful numbers are left as they are and can be interpreted without being simplified. Once you learn your life path number, you can better learn about yourself and your place in the universe.

Chapter 6: The Divining Art of Tarot

The tarot has been used as a divination tool ever since the rise of mysticism in the 18th century. It all began in Italy during the late 14th century when the card game Tarocchi was invented. It had complicated rules and striking imagery.

Occultists assigned certain meanings to every tarot image.
https://www.pexels.com/photo/close-up-shot-of-a-person-holding-tarot-cards-7181711/

Cards like the Moon, the Sun, the priestess, etc., were initially adopted from Tarocchi. Moreover, as this game continued to gain popularity across Europe, society's elites commissioned artists to create personal imagery specifically for them. Often the knight of cups, the hierophant, and other figures was based on the family who hired the artist.

During the early 18th century, European and Western occultists drew a link between Tarocchi and an Ancient Egyptian text used by gypsies in Europe. These occultists claim that the Tarot originated in ancient Egypt. However, this claim has not been supported by real evidence to this day.

Based on their observations, occultists assigned certain meanings to every tarot image. Western occultists divided the Tarocchi cards into two groups, the Major and Minor Arcana. They noticed that the Major arcana, formally known as the trump cards, use Hebrew letters found in the Kabbalah, which are magical Hebrew interpretations of the Torah. These letters are connected to certain elements, planets, or zodiac signs. After this discovery, the Major Arcana gained more evolved, richer meanings.

As for the Minor Arcana, there were slight changes made. In the 1700s, the suits were different. Both traditional and modern decks contain similar suits (swords and cups), but modern decks have replaced staves and discs with wands and pentacles.

Every image holds secret messages and codes. The meanings behind these mystical images changes depending on which cards surround them. Since the changes were integrated into tarot, they have been used as a divination tool that informs the reader of the past, present, and future. People have been using it to answer unanswerable questions and ease their worries.

Types of Tarot Decks

The Tarot of Marseilles

By the 16th century, Marseilles, France, and Italy were the tarot hubs. Later, in the 18th century, Grimaud, a French company, published the Tarot of Marseilles, a deck that became all the rage across Europe. It gained so much popularity that the company started exporting this deck to other companies. Later, cities in northern Italy and countries like Switzerland and others started to print and publish this deck.

The Tarot of Marseilles is truly remarkable because it paved the way for the modern tarot. The 18th-century occultists based their theories on this deck, and the ever-famous Rider-Waite-Smith deck's design was based on the Marseilles deck.

The Rider-Waite-Smith Tarot Deck

The Rider-Waite-Smith tarot deck is one of the most famous tarot decks to this day. It was developed by Arthur E. Waite, designed by Pamela C. Smith, and published by William Rider in 1910.

During this time, William Rider wrote The Key of the Tarot, which was published with the deck. This book was a guide to help people interpret the tarot and learn the art of picking up its energies.

The Rider deck's popularity spread like wildfire, and every tarot practitioner was using it. Today, most modern tarot decks' designs are based on the Rider pack. Many practitioners today still use the Rider deck, whether on their website or with their clients.

The Thoth Tarot Deck

Aleister Crowley developed the Thoth Tarot deck in 1944. This deck follows hermetic principles and is connected to systems such as astrology, the kabbalah, and the golden dawn. This deck is perfect for readers who want to integrate different systems as they are conducting a reading.

Cultural Decks

Modern-day tarot is based on the Marseilles and the Rider decks. The idea behind them is the same as the previous decks, but their designs are completely different. The more tarot grew in popularity, the more freedom it gained.

Though the meanings remained the same, the designs rapidly changed. Why is this important? Imagery is a powerful tool. When people see pictures that they can relate to, the energy collectively changes. Tarot is energy work, so the readings are more accurate if the energy is intensified.

Cultural decks do not have a specific design, but when you see one, you'll recognize it. These types of decks are used by people from all different nationalities and ethnicities.

They often reference elements from various cultures, and these elements vary from cultural symbols to universal references that everyone can understand. The universally referenced images convey messages that help the card reader with their interpretations.

Oracle Cards

Oracle cards are slightly different from tarot cards, but they are used in the same way. These cards also have images and often have a message written on them as well. Oracle cards are used in conjunction with tarot spreads and often help the reader give a clearer reading or support what is seen in the tarot spread. Oracle cards are widely different from one another. You can find cards that are centered around the phases of the moon, seasons, elements, astrology, fairy folk, and different themes.

Which Deck Is Suitable for You?

There is such a wide variety of tarot cards available that it can get a bit overwhelming when you are buying your first deck because you want it to be special. Still, any deck that you buy will be special since it is the first of your ever-growing collection.

Every tarot reader has a personalized system and style. As a beginner, you probably haven't settled into your own style yet. This is just the start of your journey, and it will take a bit of time to get there, so there is no need to force anything. Readings are based on intuition and introspection, so when you buy your first deck, follow your instincts. Since there is no one way to pick your first deck, here are a few pointers that can help you when you are about to purchase your first set of cards.

Connection

One of the easiest ways to pick a deck is to see which one you feel connected to the most. Take yourself to the store and browse all the different cards. After you have finished browsing, check in with yourself. See which deck you feel attracted to the most or see yourself using more than the others. Gut feelings and intuition are powerful, so listen to them.

Pick a System

Certain Tarot decks are attached to different systems. For instance, the Marseilles and Rider deck are basic decks. They have a few astrological elements, but the rest is fairly simple. On the other hand, the Thoth deck is connected to the golden dawn, astrology, and the Kabbalah. If one of these systems stands out to you, then this is your sign to purchase the deck that is connected to it.

Google Them

Another easy way to do this is to Google the decks that interest you the most. You can see what they look like on the inside. If you are a visual person, then this method will help you. After you have Googled your cards, pick the ones that call out to you the most, and you can use your intuition to help you.

Size Matters

You'll have to do a lot of shuffling when practicing tarot, so make sure that you pick a size you are comfortable handling. Tarot cards vary in size, so check the cards' size before buying them. You want to be comfortable shuffling them, especially when you are a beginner reader.

Card Attunement

One of the most significant steps that you need to cover is card attunement. This is a process by which you connect your energy with your cards so that your intuition can pick up their messages, resulting in accurate readings. It is vital that you connect with your cards whether you are a beginner or an advanced reader. Whenever you buy a new deck, you have to connect with them. There are multiple ways that you can do so if you do not know how to connect to your deck.

Quality Time

Spend time with your cards. The more you are around them, the more your energy fields intertwine. This means holding them and setting your intention to connect with them. You can sleep next to them or cover them with a garment or a necklace that you wear often. You can keep them in your hands for a while or shuffle them a bunch of times.

Journaling

You can also journal and reflect on your new cards. Hold each card in your hand, then journal about them. Pick a random card and journal about the feelings that it inspires within you. You can also set your intentions when you are journaling. You can write about how you are feeling about your new cards and state that you are connecting with them. You can also note down how it feels to connect with your deck. Emotions are strong with tarot, so make sure you use your feelings when journaling.

Meditating

Meditation is another powerful tool that can help you to connect to your cards. Find somewhere comfortable, or go to your meditation place if you have one. Then hold the cards in your hands and begin breathing and meditating. As you inhale and exhale, imagine your energetic field connecting with the cards. Envision yourself using the cards smoothly and experiencing accurate readings.

Deck Cleansing

Your tarot cards are connected to your energy, so when this card energy has been used or tarnished, it needs to be energetically cleansed. Using your cards before they have been properly cleansed is going to compromise any reading you may make. Generally, it is best to cleanse the deck before and after every reading.

This cleansing is necessary because whoever you have done a reading for was channeling your cards energetically, and they could leave their energy attached to the cards. This means that when you are doing a reading for yourself or someone else, this person's energy will still be lingering, and that is never a good thing, so make sure to cleanse your deck.

You'll encounter difficult and deep readings with yourself and others. You might do a reading for someone who is going through emotionally challenging times. If this is the case, then make sure you properly cleanse your deck before and after this reading so that you do not take this heavy energy with you.

How to Cleanse Your Deck
Smoke

Any type of incense will work when you are cleansing your deck. You can also you can use herbal smoke. Aim to use cleansing herbs like sage, rosemary, peppermint, basil, and sweetgrass. You can also use palo santo to cleanse your deck from any unwanted energies.

Visualization

This may sound bizarre at first, but *visualization* is a powerful tool. Your mind and energy field are capable of so much more than you might think. All you need to do is put the cards in front of you, close your eyes, and imagine a bright golden light entering your deck and cleansing it from the inside out. After you feel like your cards have been purified, you can begin using them.

Crystals

Crystals contain powerful energy within them. Like herbs, each crystal has a different set of properties, so look for ones that have purification energy. You can use crystals like Black Obsidian, Selenite, Black Tourmaline, Smoky Quartz, Amethyst, Rose Quartz, Citrine, Clear Quartz, Turquoise, Sodalite, and so many more. You can place any of these crystals on top of your deck and pick them up later when you feel they have been purified.

Sound

Sounds and certain frequencies have purification abilities. You can surround your deck with beautiful music or use your signing bowl and produce sounds that purify the deck's energy. You can also sing to your deck, and it can be a beautiful part of your practice. Find something that matches your style and use whatever method you are most comfortable with.

Moonlight

You can also leave your deck beneath the Moonlight. The full Moon phase is the most powerful, so you can leave your deck beneath the Moon at its peak. However, any other Moon phase will do.

Sunlight

The sunlight has healing and cleansing energies. You can set your deck beneath the Sun and return to it when you feel it has been cleaned. You can also do this when your readings have been a bit fuzzy or unclear.

Salt

Salt is a powerful cleansing tool. You can drench your deck in sea salt or regular salt. You can also set salt stones on top of your deck and use them when they have been purified.

Tips and Tricks

Grounding

If you are a beginner tarot practitioner, then grounding yourself before a reading is necessary. The tarot functions by using the energy field of the reader, so if you are not centered, then your reading can drain you. On the other hand, your energy could be scattered and not focused, which will result in an inaccurate reading. A good way to ground yourself is to sit on the floor with bare feet, take deep breaths, and set your intentions for the reading.

Utilize the Energies

Grounding techniques are a big part of the reading ritual, but sometimes you'll need something stronger when you are unable to ground yourself. You can use different tools to help you with your energy field. Try reading in nature. You can be in a garden or on the sand; both will ground you. You can also use crystals. Let's say you want to preserve your energy as you are doing a reading. In this case, you can wear crystals that protect your energy.

Use the Baby-Step Method

Interpreting tarot cards is fascinating, but it can also be overwhelming at first. As a beginner, you may be confused or flooded by all the cards and patterns you need to learn. You can prevent this by easing yourself into the process. Learn about one card each day. You can set two piles down - learned and unlearned cards. The more your learned pile grows, the more you can try creating patterns and interpreting them together. You can also try the 3-card pattern first before you delve deeper into more complex patterns.

Learn Patterns

Speaking of patterns, you'll find plenty of spreads that you can create with the cards. There are classic ones like the Celtic cross, the 3-card spread, the 5-card spread, spiritual guidance, relationship, astrological, and so many more. You can ease yourself into this by learning easy spreads, like the 1-card reading and the 3-card spread. As you practice these spreads and get more comfortable, you'll be able to take on more elaborate patterns. Later, you can create your own patterns and inquire about the cards about anything you are wondering about.

Practice

The traditional tarot deck has 78 cards and numerous spreads. You cannot expect to learn all of this overnight. It needs time and a lot of practice. You'll gradually get the hang of it the more you learn – *and the more you practice what you have learned.* The best way to practice is by yourself. Try doing a lot of readings for yourself until your reading is smooth and your intuition is sharp. Then you can start giving close friends reading to test your skills with other people.

Learn from Others

The tarot is an ancient practice, and people have been practicing it since the 18th century. So, you can imagine how it has evolved and how people have found new ways to have more accurate readings. Get some tarot books and learn how different people read their cards. Adopt anything that evokes inspiration within you until you have developed your style.

Tarot is a divination tool that has been part of people's spiritual practices for years and has helped many people by answering questions and easing worries.

The beautiful thing about tarot is that anyone can practice it; it is not an exclusive practice. If you are thinking about becoming a tarot practitioner, you need to include it in your spiritual practice.

Purchase a deck that you feel connected to or attracted to. Then cleanse it and spread them so that you can get to connect with them on a more intimate level. Do not try to rush the process; ease yourself into it and familiarize yourself with your cards one step at a time.

Now, you can start learning one card a day and familiarize yourself with different patterns. This may feel slow at first, but do not be discouraged. Your pace will increase one day at a time. Eventually, you'll find yourself conducting readings for yourself easily. Remember to ground yourself before readings and cleanse your deck before and after your readings.

Chapter 7: How to Read the Tarot

Embarking on your tarot journey must feel exciting and overwhelming all at once. You do not have to worry about this, though, because this chapter will help narrow things down for you, and you'll find where to start and how to expand your knowledge when it comes to your new practice.

There are several placements that allow you to read tarot.
https://pixabay.com/es/photos/tarot-tarjetas-tarjeta-profec%c3%ada-2114403/

We have set out a few rituals that you may want to adopt. These activities will help you gain a fresh perspective, feel calm and centered, and put your mind in the right space to do effective readings. You may feel like there are a lot of rituals to remember and go through before you start reading, but you don't have to follow all of them. They are merely pointers to help you to have a clear reading, and it is really up to you to decide whether you would like to include them in your practice or not.

Remember, at the end of the day, tarot is a highly personal practice, which means that you get to decide what it should be like for you. You'll eventually have your own style, with your own set of rituals and ways of reading. So really, there is no reason to worry about the form of your practice. Just go with the flow, and you'll find that your practice has taken on its own form and shape.

Rituals

Almost every spiritual practice has rituals, and tarot is no different. Every practitioner has a routine that they go through before listening to the cards. And, since you are a new reader, it may be best that you are introduced to different practices to decide which ones you like and will use – and which don't resonate with you.

As mentioned in the previous chapter, grounding and cleansing are vital before reading. To recap, you can ground yourself by meditating, using crystals, or sitting with nature. You can also resort to other methods when you want to ground yourself. However, if you feel like your energy is scattered, then grounding is necessary.

Cleansing is also a must. This is a practice that you simply cannot disregard. You must eliminate any energy in your cards for a clear and accurate reading. Otherwise, your readings may be off-key, and the energy that has lingered on may affect you or others negatively, so be careful.

Intuition Tuning

Tarot reading is half an understanding of symbology and half intuition. And as a beginner, you might have some of the following questions. What does this mean? Have you ever seen a little book that comes with the tarot deck? Well, this book explains what each card means. However, why do we need tarot interpreters if there is a book that clearly explains every card? Why is it a spiritual practice? What is so special about this?

It is true that every card is clearly explained. However, that is not enough. Understanding the symbols is one thing, and interpreting the cards is another. Your intuition is the tool that helps you to decode the cards. Think about it, how will a book be able to explain different spreads and patterns with the cards that you drew out? A book cannot decipher this, but your intuition can.

There are various ways that you can sharpen your intuition. You can start by making meditation a daily practice. Meditation trains your mind to be quiet and listen to the subtle messages coming from your intuition.

You can also use essential oils to stimulate your third eye. Opening your third eye sharpens your intuition and helps you hear it. You can use lemon, jasmine, or sandalwood mixed with a carrier oil and rub it on your pineal gland. You can also inhale their aroma instead of putting them on your skin.

Crystals such as Rhodonite, Amethyst, Purple sapphire, Sodalite, Violet Tourmaline, and others can help clear the pathways between you and your intuition. You can spend time meditating with the crystal of your choice and setting your intentions to listen to your intuition. You can also carry these crystals with you to keep your intuition sharp. Remember, setting your intentions with spiritual work is everything.

Shuffling

Shuffling your tarot cards is a must. Firstly, it helps restore energy. Secondly, mixing the cards up as you focus your energy helps you get a good reading.

There is really no one specific way to shuffle your cards; you can do it however you like. Just remember to set your intentions and channel your energy as you do so. You can talk to your cards as you move them around. You might pose questions to the cards or ask for a reading.

Pick Your Cards

Usually, beginners have a difficult time picking out a tarot card. They are unsure how to do it and often doubt themselves and their intuition. If you have been going through this doubt yourself, know that it is okay and that it is a normal part of the journey.

Picking out your cards will get easier the more you practice. You can start by spreading them out after the shuffling. Ideally, they should be faced down when they are spread out. Now you can start connecting with your intuition and feelings. Try to feel which cards are calling out to you. The cards you feel most attracted to are the ones that are supposed to be in your reading.

Spreads

By now, you are familiar with tarot spreads or patterns. However, to paint a clearer picture, this section will explain what spreads are and the types of patterns that you can use.

To put it simply, a tarot pattern is a way of placing the cards chosen in a certain manner. For instance, one card can be on top of four other cards. This is one of the five-card spreads that you can use. You can put three cards next to each other, and this is known as the three-card spread.

The Celtic Cross

The Celtic Cross is one of the most popular spreads. It features ten cards, each representing a different element or factor. So, begin by shuffling your cards while focusing on your question. Then spread the cards and pick ten of them.

The first card should be placed in the center. This card is called the querent, and it represents you.

The second card should be placed horizontally on top of the first card, creating a cross. It is called the block. From the name, this card represents the problem or the situation that is stopping you.

The third card should be placed beneath the central card. This one is known as the root. It identifies the cause of your problems.

The fourth card should be placed next to the left of the central card. This card is known as the recent past, and it shows you what has been taking place lately in your life.

The fifth card, or "Possibilities," goes above the central card. It represents different options or possibilities around you in the present.

The sixth card goes next to the right of the central card. This represents where you are going or where you are headed based on your present situation. It can also show you what you need to do to achieve the desired outcome.

To place the seventh card correctly, imagine there is a line forming next to card six. Add card number seven at the bottom of this line. This card represents how you see yourself and your power in the present moment.

Place card number eight on top of the seventh. This card represents your current environment and the kinds of influences that might be affecting you right now.

The ninth card goes on top of the eighth. This card will reveal your feelings, hopes, fears, and everything in between.

Finally, the tenth card goes on top of the ninth. This card will give you a picture of the outcome based on the current situation.

Three Cards

The three-card spread is one of the simplest patterns that you could use. Usually, beginners practice with this pattern because it is the easiest to use, and it introduces them to the concept of patterns in general and how they can use more complex ones.

Basically, any three cards next to each other is a three-card spread. You can ask the cards about anything and pick out three cards that will give you your answer. Here are a few sample patterns, but remember that you can create your own.

Situation, Action, Outcome

Yes, Maybe, No

Past, Present, & Future

Embrace, Accept, Let go

You, the Person in question, the Relationship

The problem, Cause, Solution

Mind, Body, Spirit

Other Patterns

Spreads are endless in tarot. There is really no one way to do it, and readers continue to create their own patterns every day. You can make up any variation that you think will best fit your question. Here are a few spreads that you might like:

Relationship Spreads
Four Cards
Your feelings

Other person's feelings

Relationship pros

The future of your relationship

Six Cards
Current Situation

Reasons to stay

Reasons to leave

Your feelings should you stay

Your feelings should you leave

Advice

Career
Five Cards
Dream job

Path to dream job

Your unique qualities

Assistance

What should you focus on right now

Six Cards
Your goal

Your challenges

What is it taking from you?

What is it adding to you?

What does your job give you?

Factors that affect you

Shadow Reading

Ten Cards

What is my shadow self like?

What are you trying to communicate to me?

What am I blinded to?

How do I ignore your messages?

How can I heal you?

When were you born?

Which lost part of me do you represent?

What are you trying to teach me?

How can I understand myself better through you?

Interpretation

Traditional Reading

Traditional reading means sticking to what everyone knows about tarot and using that to figure out what the card means. If you would like to read the tarot traditionally, then you'll need to do a lot of reading and learning. Look for different books written by authoritative authors and soak up their knowledge. Take note of how they interpret the cards according to the traditional way.

The drawback of this kind of reading is its lack of flavor. It is not original and is empty of style and identity. Sticking to traditional tarot can ease your worries about interpreting the cards correctly, but this way, you'll be erasing your own voice from the reading.

Intuitive Reading

Intuitive reading means interpreting the tarot by listening to your intuition. Intuitive reading does not ignore the traditional meanings of the cards. On the contrary, it takes them into account. However, it does not rely heavily on the traditional meanings of the cards. The best way to do an intuitive reading is to mix the traditional meanings with your intuition, resulting in an accurate and spiritual meaning.

This kind of reading can be tricky at first, but the more you are in tune with your intuition, the more you'll be at ease when reading.

You will notice that your confidence reaches new heights the more you practice.

Symbols

Symbology is key in Tarot. Pick any random card right now, and you will notice various symbols on one card, whether it is a lake, moon, chains, lantern, castle, etc. You can read your cards by interpreting the symbols they have. This goes into intuitive reading because it is not enough to rely on symbols alone. Still, symbols are powerful when properly understood.

You need to be well-read to understand the different symbols. You can try to learn a few symbols every day and note down your newly found knowledge so that you do not forget. You can check out these symbols in your tarot books or be aware of the popular symbols around us.

Reversed Reading

Have you ever noticed reversed cards in a tarot reading? There is a reason these cards are flipped, but the message really depends on the interpreter. If you want to experiment with reversed cards, you need to intuitively flip a few cards here and there and then shuffle the whole deck. This will result in a few reversed and upright cards.

Now you can begin picking out your cards and interpreting your cards. You'll read the reversed cards in the same way you read the upright ones, just in reverse. For instance, the hermit represents chosen solitude, soul-searching, inner guidance, and inner wisdom. When it is in reverse, it means isolation, pushing others away, and loneliness.

Additional Tips

Tarot Journaling

Keeping a tarot journal will become a powerful tool in your arsenal. The more you write down your readings or take notes from them, the more confident you'll become in your craft. You'll be able to see a pattern of how your intuition works, which will make you trust it even more. This habit also allows you to connect deeply with your craft. Being connected to your tarot deck makes your readings more powerful and soul-felt.

However, be careful that no one else touches your deck if you plan to build this deep connection with it. Energy work is subtle yet powerful. You do not want anyone else's energy to have a negative impact on your energy or your deck.

Tarot and Oracle Cards

Now, this area is completely up to you - but you can mix tarot cards with oracle cards. You can do this by shuffling your tarot deck and picking out as many cards as you see fit. Then shuffle your oracle cards and place them near your tarot cards. Then you can begin to interpret what the cards are telling you.

This mix gives you more insight and more room to interpret things that you did not see before. The more room you give the cards for them to speak to you, the louder they will be. So, try it out and see if this is something that helps you or if you would like to include it in your craft.

Mix Your Decks

Mixing your decks is similar to adding oracle cards to your tarot reading. You can do this by purchasing a couple of decks that have attracted your attention. Then, after you have finished cleansing them and connecting with them, you can mix them together.

Shuffle each deck separately, then pick out as many cards as you like from each deck. Proceed to read them together. How does this help? Well, each deck offers different imagery and various symbols. This can help you to see underlying factors that you have not seen before, and this will give you more insight.

After you have finished, make sure you thank the cards and put them back in their original deck. Be careful not to mix them up together, and, of course, cleanse them once you have finished using them.

Ambiance

Creating an ambiance for yourself helps you get in the zone. For instance, if you are used to reading with soft light and music, then every time these elements are around you, you'll find yourself focused and centered.

You can have incense, candles, or crystals around you. You could have a tarot table set up in a section of your house or a whole room that is dedicated to your readings. You can read in nature or indoors. It is really up to you, but whatever you choose, make sure that it enhances your focus and calms you down.

Reading the cards is not as complicated as it seems. It might seem like a lot at first because there are 78 cards in one deck and a lot of patterns that you'll need to learn. You'll have to learn the meaning of each card, as well as what it means when it is surrounded by different cards. There is absolutely no reason why you should not feel overwhelmed at first. The learning journey is rich with new knowledge that you'll have to soak up to become a practitioner.

However, your intuition is a powerful tool that makes the learning journey much easier than it may initially seem. Sharpen your intuition as you learn new meanings and decipher various symbols. Do not forget to practice grounding and trust your intuition because it will help you read with clarity and accuracy.

Finally, do not be afraid to mix it up. This is a personal journey, and it is only natural that you develop your own unique style when you interpret the cards. So, it is really up to you if you want to include different tarot decks or oracle cards in the same reading. You cannot have a "wrong" style when it comes to this beautiful and spiritually insightful practice. Happy readings, dear tarot reader.

Chapter 8: Palmistry and Palm Reading

It's human nature to be curious about the unknown, particularly about what the future holds in store. This curiosity has led to the invention of numerous predictive sciences and techniques. Divination techniques like numerology, astrology, and palmistry have always attracted people, whether in days gone by or in modern times. Palmistry, or the art of palm reading, is an ancient technique that helps determine one's personality traits and possible predictions of what their future holds. Also sometimes known as chiromancy, the art of palm reading is not bound to a singular culture, religion, or region. Instead, it has moved all over the world, passed down from generation to generation. Due to its origin, the practice has many versions used to analyze the various lines and features displayed on the palm of a hand. A palm reader is a name often denoted to those who read the patterns in palms, and a palmist is also a given name, but the actual name for someone who dabbles in the art is a *chirologist.*

Palm reading requires attention to the details found in the lines and groves.
https://pixabay.com/es/photos/mano-l%c3%adneas-cauce-palm-piel-5219349/

Out of all the divination practices, the art of palm reading is considered the most highly regarded, although it's a bit challenging to master. Hands, particularly palms, are seen as valuable portals that can shed light on a person's characteristics and even predict their future. There are a few factors to weigh in to make the complete analysis. However, understanding the basics of palmistry is not as difficult as you might think. And once you learn the ropes of this powerful predictive technique, you'll be on your way to mastering this art in no time. This chapter will provide a detailed guide to palm reading, its history, theories, and techniques.

History of Palmistry

There's a general uncertainty about the origins of palmistry. While many people believe that it originated in India and spread elsewhere from there, others argue that it was started in ancient Greece by the great scientist Aristotle. The art was then passed on to Alexander the Great, who took a keen interest in the subject and practiced it in the hands of his soldiers. Moving further into the future, Hippocrates also employed palm reading techniques to diagnose diseases. While it may have started in Ancient Greece, it soon spread to India, China, Persia, Egypt, and many more countries.

The rapid spread of this divination method can be attributed to the fact that people were fascinated by the thought of predicting the future, and with so many predictions being accurate, there was no shortage of believers. Today, palmistry is still as widespread as before, if not more so. Modern palmists often relate their readings to psychology as well to provide a more in-depth analysis.

Palm Reading Guide

Although there are numerous versions of palm reading techniques all over the world, there are some steps and theories that are followed universally. A good chirologist thoroughly analyzes every line, feature, mount, bump, and intersection on the palm. While a simple analysis can be made by identifying and interpreting the major lines, a more thorough reading would require you to study the shape of the hand, identify the different mounts and what they represent, and finally, interpret the meaning of the major and minor lines and intersections present on the palm. Furthermore, you should also characterize the shape and size of each finger present on the hand and make classifications based on the color of the palm.

Choose a Hand

Before you can start interpreting the meanings behind various features present on the palm, you need to select a hand to analyze. For women, the right hand is considered to be what you're born with, whereas the left hand portrays your accomplishments throughout your life, and, for men, the opposite is true. Some prefer selecting your dominant hand as a representation of the present and past, while the other hand represents what is to come.

Opinions on this subject vary, but most experts believe that it's necessary to analyze both hands to reveal the natural personality and future potential. The readings reveal how a person is and how they can use their characteristics and potential in this lifetime.

Determine the Shape of the Hand

The human personality is a pretty complicated mixture of characteristics and attributes. Similar to how astrology classifies various attributes with the time and place of one's birth to elemental signs, palmistry also relates the four elements with one's hand shape. Each hand type directly correlates with one of the four elements: water, fire, earth, and water. However, your astrological or birth chart readings may not always align with your palm readings. So, even if you have a fire sign in your birth chart, the shape of your hand may reveal you to be a water sign, which may signify the complex nature of your personality. Each hand shape has specific features and traits associated with it, as listed below:

The Earth Hand

Like the earth, they are firmer and more solid. The palm is more or less a *square shape*, with short fingers. The skin of the palm is thick, tough, and ruddy in color. Palm length and finger length are roughly the same. People with earth hands are practical, energetic, responsible, and humble. They are usually good leaders and great at managing people and executing instructions. Earth hands show people who are to be relied on and offer security - they do not become absorbed in themselves and their own problems and are a person who can be leaned no in times of need.

They are not very ambitious at times and are usually comfortable with a moderate lifestyle and basic necessities. Jobs that require minimal complex operations are most suitable for these people. They're not the kind to make grand romantic gestures; they are happiest with simple romance. Those with earth hands can develop breathing ailments and are not great with heights.

The Air Hand

Air hands are not fleshy and have more squat palms that are not as round as other elements - the skin is often dry. This hand type signifies intelligent, curious, and smart individuals who are good at analyzing situations and adapting to change quickly. They have an innate desire to explore things and are often gifted with a highly creative side. People with air hands yearn for a romantic lifestyle and are usually social butterflies. This leads air hands to be less focused than others, and if they do not have enough stimulation in life, they can become bored or on edge.

The Water Hand

These hands are longer and lither - both the palm and the fingers. Longer fingers generally lead water hands to be players of instruments. Water hands are softer than their counterparts, and they can be oily or clammy too. They know how others are feeling and often feel the same. Water hands are in touch with feelings, intuition, and seeing beyond the physical realm. These individuals are fueled by kindness and creativity. Mostly introverts (though there can be exceptions), people with water hands are very emotional and get hurt easily. This can cause some personal stress and issues. Their interest is in all things beautiful and creative; thus, many are huge art lovers.

The Fire Hand

Fire hands have lengthened palms with shorter fingers. The fingers are usually shorter in length than the palm. The palm itself has a pinkish or ruddy coloring with defined mounts and creases. Traits associated with fire hands people include an energetic nature, smart, diligent, optimistic, and self-confident. People with fire hands are usually extroverts by nature and are often the life of the party. These individuals love a colorful life and never let a moment get dull. However, they can be somewhat lacking in compassion and may make bad decisions driven by their desires.

Identify the Mounts

Identifying the type of hand is only the beginning. The next step is to study the palm in more detail. You are looking for the mounts – the fleshy areas on the palm. We can look to the planets for more information on our mounts.

The mounts that seem rounded and elevated represent the stable nature of the attributes associated with the respected mount. Whereas sunken mounts depict the individual's weaknesses or vulnerabilities in regard to specific attributes. Furthermore, mounts that are extremely prominent or elevated reveal a person's dominant traits, which can impact their lives and personality positively or negatively. To observe your mounts, cup your hand just a little and notice which ones are protruding and which ones are not.

Outer Mars, Inner Mars, and Plain of Mars

You cannot look at palms without utilizing Mars. Mars is the planet (and god) of war, and you'll find aggression, resilience, and temperament in the mounts when you read them. Look for the

Inner Mars above the thumb, and use the mount to discover the strength of the individual. You'll also find the Outer Mars on the palm, and this will tell you the persistence and emotional intelligence of the individual. Finally, the plain of Mars, which lies at the lower center of the palm, signifies how the qualities mentioned above are balanced together.

Mount of Jupiter

Look to this mount for passions, dreams, confidence, and authority. It is located at the base of the index finger, right above the inner Mars region. The mount itself signifies a connection to the divine and the spiritual realm. If this region is prominent, it shows that you're dominant, confident, and maybe somewhat arrogant. If this region is lacking, it means you lack confidence.

Mount of Saturn

Located at the base of the middle finger right next to the mount of Jupiter, this is associated with wisdom, intelligence, fortitude, and responsibility. This region exposes whether or not a person has integrity and the ability to take responsibility when things get bad. A too-prominent mound shows that you're stubborn and cynical. And, when there is not a mound, the person is shallower and more unorganized.

Mount of Apollo

Find this mount under the ring finger and beside the Saturn mount. Apollo (the sun) relates to happiness, optimism, and vigor. The Apollo mount also shows the artistic side of a person and their potential in life. If the sun mount is excessively prominent, it means you're extravagant and quick-tempered. A low mount means you lack imagination and creativity.

Mount of Luna

The mount of Luna is located at the end of the palm, towards the side of the pinky finger. The name comes from the moon goddess, and you'll find empathy, knowledge, wisdom, creativity, daydreams, and divination in this mount.

Mount of Mercury

The mount of Mercury is located right below the pinky finger and is attributed to an individual's wit, charm, social skills, and adaptability. This region represents if the individual is resourceful or not and how their mind works strategically. If it's protruding, you talk too much. A lack of a mount of Mercury can signify shyness.

Mount of Venus

Look for this mount at the root of the thumb. You'll use the mount of Venus to discover the sexuality, sensuality, and amorous nature of the person. The type of mount will show how drawn people are to the person and how deep of a connection they can form.

Identify the Major Lines

The most important aspect of palm reading is interpreting the palm's folds, creases, or lines. While numerous lines are present in the palm of a hand, only the main ones are the focus for narratives and predicting future happenings. Several features come into play when focusing on the major lines. Their length, curvature, and depth all make a difference in the final interpretation. It's crucial to observe minute details of the lines, where they begin and end, where they intersect, and which mounds they cross. Each of these details plays a part in the complete interpretation of a reading.

The Life Line

Located above the mount of Venus or the base of the thumb, the life line is the one that arches slightly and extends around the thumb. Contrary to popular belief, the length of the life line does not predict how long you'll live. Instead, it reveals your health and physical fitness. The depth of the line depicts the fullness of your experiences, whereas the length reveals the influence of other people on your life. The life line can be displayed on one's palms in the following ways:

A large arc that is on full display - the individual is full of life and vibrancy

A long life line - signifies the person's physical fitness and athletic nature

A slight arc toward the base of the palm - the individual might have fatigue often

Multiple life lines - meaning the individual is full of life, optimistic, and happy.

The start of the life line is frayed (near the wrist) - signifies the early life sickness a person might have had

The end of the lifeline is disrupted or broken (near the index finger) - the individual should pay attention to their health problems when they get older, as they are likely to face issues

Circle, spiral, or cut in the life line - the individual might get physically hurt

A straight line moving across the palm - an individual who is courageous and confident

The Heart Line

The heart line, or love line, is located across the palm, right under the fingers. It can be slightly arched or move straight horizontally. The heart line reveals attributes related to the heart. These can include feelings, emotions, love, lust, romance, and emotional control. The heart line is usually observed on the palm in these ways:

Straight and small - someone who is closed off from love and relationships

Lengthy line across the palm - an understanding person when it comes to relationships – they will treat others with care

A line that touches the index finger - the outlook for love is positive

A line coming into contact with the middle finger - someone who is more self-absorbed and will be like that in a relationship.

A heart line ending between the ring finger and middle finger - someone who is quick to engage in romantic relationships

A line with a lot of movement (not straight) - someone who engages in short relationships with many lovers

Circles on the heart line or broken heart lines can denote unhappiness in a relationship

The Money Line

You'll find the money line (or fate line) between the middle finger and the wrist. Also referred to as the line of destiny, this line reveals how much a person's life will be influenced by external factors out of their control. Our hands, especially our palms, will change over time, which means that our fate will change too. It represents an individual's career or fortune. The following cases can be observed for the fate line:

A life and money line that starts together - a person with a lot of confidence and believe in themselves

Double fate line - an individual with an entrepreneurial spirit who takes on more than one job at a time

Simple, straight line - a fortunate or lucky person. The person is lucky in terms of careers/money

A split money line - someone who feels the need to switch jobs or roles frequently

A short line - a person who might retire before retirement age

The Head Line

Our minds play an essential role in shaping our destiny. Thus, the head line reflects a person's intellectual capabilities and pursuits. It lies in the very center of the palm and might arc a little. Look to the head line to discover what you need to learn in life to make the best of it. You'll also find signals of intelligence here, and the line will offer insight into a person's educational pursuits and what they might pursue. Different head lines will denote very different things:

Wavy lines denote more progressive thinking and ways of adapting

Straight lines are straightforward, just like the person. They want to take the easy path through life (not in a bad way) and stick to what they know

A cut in the line can denote mental suffering or pain that needs to be broken through

Large curves in the line shows great creativity

When the head line is short, it shows a focus not on educational pursuits, and the person is more likely to find success in physical pursuits

The Marriage Line

An important line to pay attention to when completing a full reading, but a line that is often ignored, especially when the person is not in a committed relationship. It is a short line located right above the love line. It starts right under the pinky finger. The marriage line reflects a person's romantic relationships and married life. Some people have just a single marriage line, while others have multiple lines above the love line. Simply observe the clearest one.

A double marriage line - someone who might engage in multiple relationships at the same time

Several marriage lines, none clear and distinct - the person may not be happy in their married life

A short or barely visible line - it might take some time for the person to wed

A longer line and almost starches to the pinky finger - a person who has high standards when it comes to what they expect from a relationship

A line that touches the ring finger - indicates money will be abundant within a relationship

Circles or gaps in the marriage line - the couple may have to live separately for a while

If the line is split in two, it shows a potential break in the relationship, and the relationship will need extra care and attention

Although palmistry has been a long-practiced form of art, it does not yield exact answers and might not always be accurate. So, as you familiarize yourself with the various theories and features of palm reading techniques, don't lose hope if you don't get pleasant results. The real purpose of these readings is to help you get lessons regarding your life so that you can channel your energy into working harder for those parts. Moreover, let your intuition guide you when making the interpretations, and keep in mind that both hands and people can change with time. Palm readings aren't set in stone, so think of them as a way to develop insight to select the best way to move forward.

Chapter 9: Runic Divination

Runic divination is also an ancient method for predicting the future. Runes are long associated with Vikings, and they found their origin in the Scandinavian countries and also some Germanic areas. Runes were to the Vikings what the alphabet is to us, and the runic alphabet predates the Latin alphabet. During the Middle Ages, these nations used runes for recording important events, accessing spiritual wisdom, and more. The word "rune" means "secret" or "mystery," alluding to the symbols' ability to reveal information that's only understandable by people with a strong intuition. This chapter is dedicated to runic divination, discussing its history, the use of runes, the different runic alphabets, and the interpretation of runic layouts.

The use of Runes dates back to the time of the Vikings.
https://pixabay.com/es/photos/runas-adivinaci%c3%b3n-runa-magia-4267425/

History of Runic Divination

Runes have a long-standing history. Norse legends confirm that the god of wisdom, Odin, discovered the runes during his ordeal at the Well of Fate. He then taught them to other deities in the Norse pantheon, which in turn, passed them onto mankind. The symbols were collected into an alphabet named Futhark, after the first two letters of the runes of the alphabet. The symbols were etched into wooden sticks, which the tribe's spiritual leaders then used as tools for accessing wisdom, protection, and strength.

Apart from being a letter in an ancient alphabet, runes also represent a universal force affecting people's lives, shaping their destiny and life path. Some are linked to the Norse gods and goddesses themselves, giving the seeker access to ask for guidance during divination. While the meaning of the runes may have slightly changed over time, they are being used to predict future events and outcomes.

How Can You Use Runes?

Runes can be used to reveal what happened in the past, what is happening around us, and what will come to be in the future. While they won't give you exact answers, they suggest how to proceed. Just like tarot cards, the reliability of the results depends on how you interpret the runes and what you decide to do after receiving an interpretation. This means that whatever answer you're looking for, you'll need your intuition to decipher it from the runes.

Since the future isn't fixed, you can also use runic layouts to change undesirable outcomes. If you're reading for yourself and you don't like the suggested result, all you need to do is change your aspect. You can do this by doing a deeper reading and learning what the best course of action is likely to be. Make the change, and the next time you do a reading, the suggested outcome will be different too.

Runic divination can be particularly helpful in situations where you have limited access to information about a possible future event or circumstance. Consulting the runes allows you to get the full picture - as long as you listen to your intuition.

Different Types of Runes

Originally runes were made from a branch of a nut tree, cut into specific lengths, and marked with symbols. Nowadays, runes are made from wood, stone, metal, bones, crystals, and pebbles. You can buy them along with a storage pouch and the white cloth they are traditionally tossed onto during the reading.

There are also different symbols or alphabets. The oldest one was called the Elder Futhark - and was in use from at least the 3rd century, although it's possible it was used even before that. This alphabet had 24 symbols divided into three Aetts or families - Freyr's Aett, Heimdall's Aett, and Tyr's Aett. Later, this alphabet was switched to the Younger Futhark, which only had symbols. Another version, the Anglo-Saxon Futhorc, had 33 runes - and it was an adaptation, so it could be translated to Old English.

The Meanings of Each Runic Symbol
Elder Futhark

Freyr's Aett:

Ruling over fertility, peace, sunshine, and peace, this aett shows you how to stay grounded in the material world.

Fehu ᚠ - Translated as "cattle" or "wealth," fehu is associated with abundance, hope, luck, and prosperity. Apart from material gain, it can also indicate good social status.

Uruz ᚢ - Translated as "ox." The ox is strong, brave, resilient, has vitality, is persistent, and works hard. The ox rune can signify health in an individual.

Thurisaz ᚦ - Known as the giant or Thor's hammer, this rune represents a challenge, protection, and power to direct one's energy to destruction, defense, or even cleansing if needed.

Ansuz ᚨ - Translated as "message," this is the rune of revelation, communication, insight, messages, signs, wisdom, inspiration, and knowledge obtained from divine or spiritual sources.

Raidho ᚱ - Also known as a journey, this rune indicates progress, evolution, and perspective. It could be interpreted as traveling physically or as a spiritual journey.

Kenaz ᚲ - Translated as "torch," Kenaz is the rune of knowledge, enlightenment, calling, ideas, and comprehension. It may also indicate the truth that's waiting to be revealed.

Gebo ᚷ - Known as "gift" in modern English, this rune denotes generosity, gifts, assistance, or talent that you either possess or will be given in the future.

Wunjo ᚹ - A rune of protection and security, especially within a group. It can denote luck, success, prosperity, and celebration.

Heimdall's Aett:

Named after the guardian of the gods and wisdom, Heimdall's aett indicates maturity and the ability to overcome obstacles and persevere despite them.

Hagalaz ᚺ - Translated as "hail," this rune represents destruction, uncontrollable forces, the power of nature, and disasters. It also indicates inevitable and necessary changes.

Nauthiz ᚾ - Translates as "needs." The needs rune symbolizes desires, needs, survival, denial of satisfaction, arguments, restrictions, and not enough.

Isa ᛁ - Isa is the ice rune and is about patience, taking time, pausing in daily life, and delay. Just as ice blocks a stream, the rune can show a blockage of a life.

Jera ᛃ - Translated as "harvest," Jera is the rune for a conclusion, end life cycle, beginnings, growth, plentiful bounty, and the abundance of wisdom.

Eihwaz ᛇ - Known as "yew" in English, this rune symbolizes connection, sacred wisdom, and divinity. It's also associated with the cycle of life and The Tree of Life.

Perthro ᛈ - Perthro can be translated as "destiny." The rune represents fertility, female energy, fate, good fortune, mysteries, chance, and influence.

Algiz ᛉ - Translated as "elk", this rune symbolizes protection, awakening, instincts, and guardianship. It often prompts you to tap into your internal power to reach your goals.

Sowilo ᚴ - The symbol of the sun, Sowilo represents vitality, success, joy, happiness, cause for celebration, or even good health and the results of reaching your goals.

Tyr's Aett:

The aett of the Norse god Tyr represents justice, war, legacy, intuition, birth, and celebration.

Tiwaz ↑ - Translated as "victory," Tiwaz symbolizes leadership, bravery, rationality, honor, and courage. It indicates that you're capable of persevering in troubling times.

Berkana ᛒ - Berkana is the birch rune, and symbolizes fertility, birth, creativity, renewal, coming together, and new beginnings.

Ehwaz ᛗ - Translated as "horse, "Ehwaz denotes moving forward, trust, progress, loyalty, duality, animal instinct, and the need for assistance.

Mannaz ᛗ - The symbol known as "man." It represents humanity, collective spirituality, relationships, mortality, values, and identity.

Laguz ᛚ - Translated as "lake," this is the symbol of water, dreams, imagination, mystery, insight, psychic and healing abilities, and knowledge.

Ingwaz ᛦ - The rune of Fertility, Ingwaz is the symbol of variety, virtue, peace, inner growth, family, ancestry, well-being, and loose ends tied up.

Othala ᛟ - Also known as "heritage" in English, this symbol represents inheritance, legacy, values, contribution, finding out what truly matters, and communal prosperity.

Dagaz ᛞ - Translated as "dawn," this rule indicates a new day, awakening, a sense of clarity, hope, a new cycle, increased consciousness, and the possibility for a breakthrough.

Younger Futhark

Here is the meaning of the Younger Futhark runes. This list contains the 16 runes used in the first version of the Younger Futhark.

ᚠ **Fé:** Translated as "wealth," this rune symbolizes money, finances, and wealth. It can be the cause of many conflicts between family members and friends.

ᚢ **Úr:** Known as "iron" or "rain" in modern English, this rune denotes an unexpected event. It can be positive, as a blessing, or negative, as danger.

ᚦ **Thurs:** Translated to English as "giant," this rune symbolizes the Norse god Thor, who was known to be a giant person with brutal force.

ᚬ **As or Oss:** This rune literally means "one of the Æsir" (or gods). It denotes divine order, absolute truth, and divine justice.

ᚱ **Reið:** Known as "ride" in modern English, this rune symbolizes a spiritual journey. It's applied for raised awareness and spiritual growth.

ᚴ **Kaun:** Best translated as "ulcer," this rune means that one must first endure suffering to gain wisdom.

ᚼ **Hagall:** Also called "hail" in English, this rune denotes a sudden and unclear change or outcome.

ᚾ **Nauðr:** Translated as "need," this rune also signifies distress or difficulty in persevering in challenging situations.

ᛁ **Ísa or Íss:** Known as the rune for "ice," this is a symbol of self-control and the ability to remain calm.

ᛅ **Ár:** Translated to English as "plenty," this rune denotes plentiful harvest during a year.

ᛋ **Sól:** Known as the runic symbol for the sun and the goddess Sol in Germanic mythology. It also represents success and wholeness.

ᛏ **Týr:** The runic symbol of the god Tyr, also associated with victory, honor, and power.

ᛒ **Björk or Bjarkan:** Translated as "birch," this rune symbolizes the birch tree. It's also linked to the superior goddess, new life, and birth.

ᛘ **Maðr:** Known as "man" in modern English, this rune represents the first man - Mannus. It's also associated with family, planning, awareness, intelligence, and continuity.

ᛚ Lögr: Translated as "sea," it's the symbol of the vital life force and feminine energy.

ᛦ Yr: Known as "yew" in modern English, this rune symbolizes death, the underworld, and the journey between the two worlds.

Rune Casting Techniques

Before delving into the different rune-casting techniques, you should consider finding a quiet space for your practice. When you've found your quiet spot and are ready to start, sit comfortably and focus your mind. You can do this through deep breathing, meditation, or any other relaxing exercise.

Think about what question or questions you want to ask. You can also say a prayer or call upon your spiritual guide at this point. Place a rune cloth on your altar or table. You'll lay runes on this.

There are many ways to cast runes, and you can select the one that suits you the best. Your choice should always reflect your experience and the type of information you're seeking about the future. Some techniques offer in-depth knowledge about future events, while others are ideal for quick confirmation. Learn the significance of each rune before you start attempting either spread. This also helps you become more confident in relying on your gut feeling. You can do this by simply picking up the runes one by one, reading up on their meaning, and contemplating how they resonate with you. Once you have this information, you'll be ready to do the layouts below.

The Three Rune Layout

If you are a rune-casting novice, this layout is the easiest to understand and will help you to move on to other types of casting. However, even experienced practitioners can use it to consult on simple matters. It's recommended to ask only one or two questions. Here is how to cast it:

With your question in mind, select three runes from the bag and put them on the cloth.

You'll be reading them from left to right.

Rune number 1 indicates your overall situation related to the question.

Rune number 2 shows a possible challenge or issue related to the question.

Rune number 3 represents the best course of action to overcome the challenge.

The Five Rune Layout

Once you've practiced divination with the first technique and learned to rely more on your intuition, you can try out the 5-rune layout. It gives you a little more insight than the previous one. Here is how to read it:

Form the question in your mind (about what is to come) and blindly choose 5 runes from the bag.

Place the first rune in the center of your divination area.

The next rune goes to the left, then one above, one below, and the final one to the right. You should have a cross shape.

You can place all the runes face up or face down. It does not matter as long as you turn them all face up at some point.

The horizontal line composed of three runes will show your timeline – what has come, what is now, and what will come.

The rune to the left indicates possible issues you need to accept and overcome.

The rune to the right shows how you can access help to overcome the issue.

The 7-Rune Layout

The 7-rune layout is another cast you can use to further develop your intuition. It also gives a little more insight into the subject you're interested in. Here is how to read the 7-rune cast:

Focusing on your intention, take seven runes out of the bag, and lay them out in a V shape.

Start reading from the top left portion of the V, go down, and then up again.

The rune at the top left of the V shows what once was.

The next rune gives you your present circumstances.

The next will show you what is still to come.

The rune at the bottom point of the V indicates actions to take to move you forward in your life.

The next rune on the upward turn shows your current emotions.

The rune two spots away from the bottom point shows your issues.

The last rune gives the possibilities for your future.

The 9-Rune Cast

9 is a sacred number in many numerologies, and casting in nines amplifies the power of the runes. It's great for exploring your position in your spiritual path and the opportunities that lay ahead of you. This cast is recommended for medium-to-difficult-level practitioners who have developed a higher level of intuition. Here is how to do it:

Consider your spiritual journey and what desires you want to fulfill while on it.

Take nine runes out of their bag and hold them in your hands.

Toss the runes out on a cloth and look at them.

The runes closer to the center of the cloth will be the most relevant to your question.

Also, pay attention to runes touching each other - as these may denote complementary influences. Runes on the opposite side of the cloth are opposing forces.

Start interpreting the runes that have their engravings face up. You can even write the message down and revisit it later.

Then, turn the ones facing down and read them as well. They often indicated outcomes you haven't considered before.

Contemplate the meaning of all runes while tapping into your intuition.

The 24-Rune Layout

This cast is usually used for annual divination practices, as it allows the querent to get an insight into what they might expect in the coming year. Here is how to read the 24-rune layout:

Spread out the runes by forming a 3x8 grid. You'll start reading from the first row, from right to left.

The first rune shows the ways you could achieve prosperity.

The second rune shows the ways to become healthier and stronger.

The third rune shows ways to defend yourself.

The fourth rune shows ways to gain wisdom, inspiration, and motivation.

The fifth rune shows the direction your life's path will most likely take during the year.

The sixth rune shows all the wisdom you can learn during the year.

The seventh rune shows all the skills you can achieve and the gifts you can have.

The eighth rune of the first row shows the ways you can achieve happiness.

The first rune of the second row (read from right to left) symbolizes changes.

The second rune denotes what you need to obtain your goals.

The third rune represents the obstacles you face when working towards your goals.

The fourth rune symbolizes all the achievements you can reach during the year.

The fifth rune illustrates the choices you'll need to make.

The sixth rune symbolizes the ways your inner skills will manifest.

The seventh rune denotes pivotal life situations you'll find yourself in.

The eighth rune of the second row symbolizes the energy guiding you on your path.

The first rune of the third row represents all your business and legal affairs.

The second rune represents the way you'll achieve growth in different areas of life.

The third rune represents friendships and family relationships.

The fourth rune represents your social status.

The fifth rune represents your emotions.

The sixth rune represents romantic and sexual relationships.

The seventh rune represents the ways you'll obtain a balance between different areas of life.

The eighth rune represents all the assets you'll gain during the year.

Chapter 10: Crystal Divination

The art of divination is so vast that you can spend your entire life learning the various parts of predicting the future. Practicing divination helps you connect with the divine and allows you to seek guidance from them regarding matters of your life. The insights gained by following these practices often originate from one's consciousness but require the use of divinatory tools to access them.

Crystals play an important role as one of the tools for divination.
https://unsplash.com/photos/p0XN3fz6l2c

Crystal divination is one of the tools used to access divine guidance and wisdom. Crystals have always played an essential role in many divinatory techniques, be it in the early ages or during modern times. Several techniques in crystal divination can be employed depending on what kind of wisdom you seek. You can either use a single technique and get your answer or choose multiple crystal divinity techniques to gain insight. Moreover, the crystals you select also depend on the type of divination technique you'd use. However, you do not need to spend a fortune on rare crystals for any technique. In fact, a proper crystal selection process should be followed when practicing particular divination techniques.

While crystal divination is not as complicated as other divination techniques, there are still a few details you should keep in mind when practicing it. So, this chapter will provide a detailed guide about the various methods of crystal divination, mainly lithomancy and crystallomancy. It also provides a list of crystals and gemstones that can be used in these processes and their interpretations.

Common Crystals Used for Divination

Crystal magic has been practiced for centuries, and while divination practices don't exactly classify as magic, there is some special power within crystals that makes them so valuable for these practices. Each type of crystal or gemstone has a unique property and symbolizes different things. Each of these crystals is also said to have specific energies or frequencies that make them unique. Crystals are used in various rituals, healing spells, and protection techniques. You can tap into the unique energies of these crystals and use them to get predictions and wisdom. To understand and interpret crystal divination readings, you need to learn what each crystal symbolizes.

Aquamarine - If you're waiting for the ideal time or opportunity, don't. Make a move right now.

Carnelian - Seek the proper balance in your life, and don't settle with whatever life gives you. Alloy happiness, love, and color into your life.

Heliotrope - Do not act impulsively. You need to learn how to persevere through this. Remain completely focused on your goals and stand your ground to achieve them.

Hematite - Don't succumb to societal pressure or what others expect of you. Don't ignore your wants and needs just for the sake of other people.

Lapis Lazuli - Pace yourself, slow down, and think through before making any decisions or acting rashly. You'll see your efforts being noticed.

Amber - Beware of what you're giving up and consider if you're getting anything from the transaction. Know what you truly want and make a decision based on that.

Clear Quartz - New information will be revealed, which will bring you clarity. Simply stay focused on your goals, retain your honesty, and you'll soon have a fresh perspective.

Malachite - Move on from what you are holding onto and concentrate on what you want and need.

Citrine - Communicate your thoughts with honesty and integrity, and you'll have a positive response. Peace and prosperity are in your future.

Amazonite - You need to take a strong stance on your beliefs now that your life is changing. Right now is the time for a fresh start and new adventures.

Moonstone - Don't be scared to speak the truth and convey your real feelings. Just go with the flow and try not to force or block anything.

Rose Quartz - It's time to forgive yourself for past mistakes and learn not to take the blame for others' mistakes as your own. Find support from those around you.

Pyrite - Be observant of any changes in attitude or deception that might take place. There is more than what can only be seen, and you should look deeper.

Labradorite - You might need a change of circumstances to achieve your goals, but be careful what you wish for, as it might not be good for you.

Blue Lace Agate - You'll need to communicate about the issue soon, and it is essential that you open up and share your true feelings.

Tiger's Eye - You should expect good news, new beginnings, and successes. However, you'll need focus and confidence to achieve this.

Unakite - You may be feeling uncertain, but going backward won't help and will only cause your problems to repeat themselves.

Tree Agate - Get to the root of your issues, and begin strengthening your roots. You'll find answers there.

Snowflake Obsidian - You're soon going to gain clarity about a situation, but you'll need to make the right choice.

Rutilated Quartz - You'll see everything coming together soon, but don't hesitate to reach out to your loved ones for help.

Depending on the crystal divination technique you follow, you'll need to choose single or multiple crystals. Once you've chosen the crystals and gemstones of your choice, you'll need to cleanse their energies before using them in a ritual. Once they're cleansed, they will need to be infused with your intention for the process.

Crystal Divination or Lithomancy

Lithomancy is a fortune-telling approach involving throwing crystals and interpreting information based on where they land. It's a pretty complicated technique and requires complete focus to master it. However, once you master it, you'll be making expert readings in no time. Although the use of stones is common practice for lithomancy techniques, crystal divinity techniques use crystals and gemstones for readings. Lithomancy can be dated back over 5,000 years, and evidence has been found for it in Persia. Most things change over time, and Lithomancy is no different - it has been adapted by many cultures, including the Romans, Egyptians, and Greeks. Today, the technique is still used by a large number of people to get insight into their future. The process of lithomancy involves the following steps:

Choose the Stones

To start with the lithomancy ritual, you'll first have to get together a crystal set of all the essential gemstones and crystals. To choose the ones suitable for you, refer to the crystal property tables at the end of this chapter. Once you have your set, you'll start to become familiar with them. It's best to use a combination of 13 crystals at a time and then replace them with every session. Pick out the crystals that resonate most with you, or embody the characteristics you're looking for.

Create a Casting Area

Once you've collected the casting stones, it's time to create the casting area where the technique will be performed. Be careful of your casting area – you'll prepare it physically, but you must also prepare it spiritually. If you carry around a lot of negative energy, you'll be stunted in your casting. Mark the area of casting by placing ropes around the area, laying out a cloth, or pouring salt to mark the boundaries.

If you are using cloth to mark your casting area, the most common cloth is black silk – more than being just a demarcation of boundaries, black silk is an object of ritual within Lithomancy. Failing that, you can mark the casting area with Himalayan salt. Do this by spreading a fine trickle of salt to form a circle the size of a basket. You'll need to cleanse the casting space by using smoke to remove any negative energies within the space.

Cast the Stones

Casting the crystals will be the major part of this divination process and will ultimately decide what readings you get. You'll need to empty your mind of any negative thoughts and feelings and put your complete focus on the task at hand. For this process, you'll need the following:

Gemstones or crystals

A silk cloth or mat

A bowl of water

First, you need to clean the gemstones and remove any negative energies they might have picked up. Do this by dipping the crystals in the bowl of water and imagining all the negative energies leaving the crystal. Carefully take the crystals out of the water and dry them off with a spare cloth.

Next, gather the casting stones between the palms of your hands, and position your hands about two to three inches above the casting area. Shut your eyes and take a deep breath in and out, in and out. Clear out your head, and remove every thought that's on your mind. Once your mind is blank and you feel calm, bring your hand close to your heart, and focus on the question at hand. Ask the universe or guides to help answer your question. Finally, drop the stones onto the surface while keeping your eyes closed.

Once you open your eyes, you'll see a pattern formed by the crystals. Any gems that have fallen outside the casting space should be considered irrelevant to your question. The crystals inside the casting space will convey what the universe is trying to tell you. The crystal closest to the center of the space will be the main indicator to answer your question. Other crystals will represent any other advice you should take into consideration. However, if no stones fall into the casting area, you'll have to repeat the process and possibly rephrase your question.

Interpret the Results

The final step of the process will be to interpret the results of your reading. This is also a crucial step requiring deep concentration and a good understanding of the meanings of each gemstone. Your casting area has different sections, and each one signifies the relevance of the crystals that fall into it. For instance, if the crystal is dropped into the inner side of the casting circle, it will significantly impact your overall reading.

Whereas the gem that lies on the outermost section of the casting space will be of little importance. To make an interpretation, you'll need to connect the meanings and representations that each gemstone is associated with and connect them with their level of significance based on where they land. So, you'll end up with a clear and precise answer to your question/s.

As a lithomancy practitioner, keeping a journal tracking every reading is good practice. This will help you interpret your readings faster and make it easy for future interpretations. So, whether you're interpreting your own reading or someone else's, make sure to track the various interpretations. Other ways to interpret the casting stones include:

Once you've cast the stones, remove the crystals that have fallen out of the casting boundary and close your eyes once again. Focus on your question again and pick a stone from the casting space. This is the stone that answers your question.

Another method is the triple stone method, where you have to pick three casting stones from the casting space, one by one. The stones represent the past, present, and future.

Alternatively, Use a Lithomancy Chart

Once you've had enough practice with the basic stone casting techniques, you can move on to more complicated processes, including a lithomancy chart. Using one will give a much more detailed interpretation of your readings. To use a lithomancy chart while casting stones, replace the casting mat or silk cloth with the lithomancy chart.

There are a few ways to design a lithomancy chart, the most common being a combination of three wheels, each divided into twelve sections. The wheels are directly related to the astrological signs relevant to your life: physical, emotional, spiritual, and more. When you cast the stones, you'll then be able to read them based on what each one denotes. For instance, if the aquamarine crystal lands on the career section of the chart, and you're currently struggling to decide whether or not to change jobs, this would be your sign to make a move for it.

Another method to make a lithomancy chart is to make the exact same number of sections as your crystals. Then, close your eyes and place a crystal on each section instead of throwing them randomly. This will provide you with insight into every aspect of your life, contrasting with the casting method, where multiple crystals could land on a single section. However, some people prefer the throwing method because sometimes you might need insight into one aspect of your life more than the others.

Once you're done with the casting process and interpreting the readings, the next step is to act on the insights you've gleaned. For instance, if you've obtained a negative reading, you need to take the necessary precautions and advice that were foretold to avoid any bad luck coming your way. On the other hand, if you get a positive reading, you can sit back and relax.

The best course of action after reading is to plan for the future accordingly because our choices in the present have a huge impact on how our future is shaped. Remember that the art of lithomancy is simply a tool to help you figure out the course of action. However, it is not set in stone, and the final decision is always up to you.

Crystal Ball Reading or Crystallomancy

Crystallomancy or crystal ball reading is another method of crystal divination that is popular to see into the future. The technique uses crystals shaped into spheres to make predictions about the future. Although you can use any kind of crystal, the most commonly used one for this method is clear quartz. Crystal ball reading might come naturally to a select few, but most have to work at the process.

Crystallomancy (crystal ball reading) first requires you to form a bond with the crystal. This means proper care of your crystal ball and not only a spiritual bond. Be sure to keep the ball clean and overlay it with a silk cloth when it is not in use. When using the ball, treat it respectfully, and store it well. This way, its energy will remain pure and personal to you. It is best to use the crystal ball when your head is free from negative thoughts and you have a complete focus on the task.

To begin scrying, follow these simple steps:

Take a light source (Candle, lamp, or torch) and place it to the side of the crystal ball. This is done to ensure that the light does not interfere with the image being formed in the crystal. Turn off all other lights in the room.

Close your eyes and bring the intended question to your mind. Take three deep breaths before opening your eyes.

Stare into the crystal until your gaze starts to drift, and you have the feeling of being both awake and not awake. Do not focus on the ball, but keep your gaze on it. After a while, some images will start to appear in the ball.

These images will not necessarily be clear and might not even make sense at the moment. Plus, most of these images will be symbolic in nature and will only make sense when you relate them to your current circumstances.

Once you've clearly understood what you observed in the crystal ball, note it down in your scrying journal. You could also simply scribble the vision down onto the journal and try to make sense of it later.

Crystal Cleansing Tips

Before you can practice any divination techniques with your crystals, you must cleanse them of any negative energies they might have picked up. This ensures that they work in harmony with your intentions and that the process goes smoothly. Some ways to cleanse your crystals include:

Take a bowl of clean water and add Himalayan pink salt or sea salt to the bowl. Stir the mixture until the salt dissolves, and then slowly dip the crystals into the water. Allow the crystals to soak for a little bit before taking them out and drying them off.

Another method is to place the crystals directly in the sun. The sunlight is said to clear away any negative energies and will recharge the crystals with pure energy.

Crystal divination is a fascinating way to get insights into the future. It has been around for centuries and has gained popularity over time. The process usually gives good results and accurate descriptions of the future. However, you should remember that it is simply a tool to help figure out the best plan of action for your future and does not actually determine what it is.

Bonus: Glossary of Terms

This last chapter contains some of the terminology most often used across the different divination methods mentioned in the book. You can use it as a reference whenever you feel the need to revisit information about a specific term.

Air Hands: Bony hands with protruding knuckles belonging to curious and analytical people with good communication skills.

Air Signs: Gemini, Libra, and Aquarius.

Altar: A sacred place where divinations and other acts of magic are performed.

Angles: Ascendant: the first cusp, Innum Coeli: the cusp of the fourth, Descendant: the cusp of the seventh, and Midheaven: the tenth cusp. All houses of the zodiac.

Ascendant: The rising sign that is apparent at the time of a person's birth on the eastern horizon.

Aspects: The relationships the planets make with each other when traveling in their orbits around the sun.

Astrology: The science of determining future events and experiences based on the position of celestial bodies at the time and place of one's birth.

Aura: The field of electromagnetic energy surrounding a person's body.

Binding: Restricting, focusing, or combining energies of several magical objects and tools.

Blueprint: An overall makeup of one's personality, reflected in their name, the numbers associated with their life, and life path.

Cardinal Signs: The signs associated with season changes:- Aries (winter-spring), Cancer (spring-summer), Libra (summer-autumn), and Capricorn (autumn-winter).

Chakras: Major energy points in the body through which the vital life force can be accessed and manipulated.

Circle: A sacred space created for the protection of the diviner during their practice.

Challenge Numbers: Numbers represent events, circumstances, and situations designed to help you prepare for large and challenging opportunities in life.

Channel: Communicating messages between different sources, worlds, and spiritual planes.

Charm: An object enriched with magical properties like protection, added strength, etc.

Clairsentience: The ability to use multiple senses to receive messages during divinatory and other practices.

Clairvoyance: The ability to clearly visualize images related to past, present, or future events.

Cornerstone: A person's strongest trait, approach to finances, or essence of their name, represented by the first letter in their first name.

Crystal Ball: An object made of crystals with magical properties, which allows you to predict future events.

Cusp: The margins of the zone represented by a zodiac house and the degree beginning at one sign and ending at another.

Descendant: Sitting opposite the ascendant is the cusp of the zodiac's seventh house.

Divinistic Dream Interpretation: Predicting the future by interpreting answers you get in your dreams after consulting Tarot cards and other divination tools.

Earth Hands: Firm and fleshy hands belonging to grounded, logical, and practical **persons.**

Earth Signs: Virgo, Capricorn, and Taurus.

Elder Futhark: An alphabet denoted by symbols that was developed by the people who inhabited Scandinavia, parts of Britain, and some smaller regions of Europe.

Electional Astrology: A branch of astrology that involves choosing preferred times for important events.

Elements: Water, Fire, Air, and Earth – each related to three zodiac signs.

Empath: A person drawn to other people's feelings and aligns their own according to what they pick up from others.

Emphatic Aspects: Aspects that align the energies of two planets with one another, like Conjunction or Opposition.

Fate Line: The line running up and down your palm that tells you what the future has in store.

Feminine Signs: Feminine signs are more receptive to negative energy – Pisces, Virgo, Scorpio, Taurus, Cancer, and Capricorn.

Fire Hands: Hands with distinctive creases and mounds - belonging to individuals with a confident, industrious and passionate nature.

Fire Signs: Leo, Aries, and Sagittarius.

Fixed Signs: Taurus, Leo, Scorpio, and Aquarius.

Frequency: The levels of energy projected towards people, objects, and situations in your environment.

Glyphs: Symbols denoting planets, astrological signs, luminary bodies, aspects, and constellations.

Grounding: Rooting yourself to the physical world to increase focus during divination or other magical acts.

Guide: An entity that provides guidance for personal growth and awareness.

Head Line: The line in the center of your palm - represents intellectual curiosity and personal goals.

Heart Line: The line above the headline - is associated with relationships, emotions, and other matters of the heart.

Holistic: Natural healing methods encompassing techniques to cure ailments of mind, body, and soul.

Houses: The 12 zones of the elliptical space across the sky, ruling over specific areas of life depending on the time of birth.

Inner Mars: Located above the thumb, this is the part of the hand representing aggression.

Insight: Using intuition to access and analyze information relevant to the question.

Intuition: Also called protective sight, it is the ability to raise yourself to an elevated state of psychic awareness.

Invocation: Calling upon a guide for assistance to decipher psychic messages.

Karma: The sum of past actions with negative consequences to your current life.

Karmic Debt: The four numbers (13, 14, 16, 19) represent the debt given to souls who must face karma to correct their past mistakes.

Karmic Lessons: Lessons every soul learns during each life cycle.

Life Line: Is found below the head lid on the palm and deals with major events in life: experiences, health, values, and morals.

Lifepath: Also called the destiny number, determines a person's intellect and important lessons to learn before moving on to the next life cycle.

Luminary Objects: the Sun and the Moon.

Major Arcana: A set of 22 cards denoting the pivotal aspects of one's life, including relationships, family, career, health, and more.

Masculine Signs: Masculine signs are more receptive to positive energy. They are Aquarius, Leo, Libra, Gemini, Aries, and Sagittarius.

Master Number: Double-digit numbers like 11, 22, and 33 in one's blueprint can boost their strength and noble personality traits.

Meditation: The practice of relaxation, which results in increased focus during divinatory and other practices.

Minor c: The deck of 56 cards representing smaller or temporary influences in one's life.

Mounts: Areas of flesh on the palm that can denote areas of your life. They relate to the major planets in our solar system.

Mutable Signs: Virgo, Gemini, Sagittarius, and Pisces.

Natal Chart: Also known as a birth chart, the natal chart reveals a person's traits and possible future according to the placement of the planets at the time of their birth.

Numerology: The art of predicting one's past, present, and future based on the most important numbers in their life.

Odin: The Norse god of wisdom, magic, poetry, death, and divination, who brought the runes to the people.

Orb: The range or distance within which a planet can influence another planet.

Outer Mars: Out with Inner Mars – deals with courage, emotion, and perseverance.

Palmistry: Also called chiromancy, palmistry is the practice of predicting one's future path by looking at the lines on their palm.

Part of Fortune: The section of the natal chart denoting an aspect in which a person has a natural aptitude.

Personal Planets: Planets with a direct effect on one's personality.

Personal Year: The number determined by one's personal blueprint. It allows insight into potential events and experiences in one's future.

Pinnacle: Unique opportunities are presented at each life cycle based on a person's blueprint numbers.

Plain of Mars: The area in the center of the palm that creates an equilibrium between the Outer and Inner Mars.

Precognition: The ability to foresee future events, situations, and circumstances.

Prediction: Messages indicating future outcomes or events.

Prophecy: Prediction made by someone with a heightened ability to reveal the future.

Reading: Accessing information (through intuition and psychic abilities) that may answer the question presented by the reader.

Regression: The ability to access information relevant to the future from the past.

Runes: Symbols with magical properties - used for divination, protection, and other magical purposes.

Rune Casting: The practice of interpreting the meaning of runes for divinatory purposes.

Runic Alphabet: Also known as futhark, an ancient alphabet consisting of runes instead of letters.

Quadrants: Groups of houses, beginning with the first, fourth, seventh, and tenth zodiac houses.

Querent: The person who presents the question about the future.

Retrograde: Apparent backward motion of a planet in relation to the Earth, resulting in the planet's negative influences on people's lives.

Scrying: Using a crystal ball (or another reflective material) to look into the future.

Speculum: A magical object used for scrying.

Sun Line: The line from the base of the hand to the pinky finger that symbolizes fame and fortune, how we are perceived in public, and what we will leave behind.

Sun sign: A person's sun sign denotes the house in which the sun resided during the time of their birth.

Synastry: A specific sublet of relationship astrology.

Tarot: A deck of 78 cards used to predict future events.

Tarot Reading: Interpreting the meaning of individual tarot cards or tarot spreads.

Waning Moon: The phase between the full moon and the new moon.

Water Hands: Hands are soft to the touch, denoting awareness of emotions, psychic abilities, and intuition.

Water Signs: Scorpio, Pisces, and Cancer.

Waxing moon: The phase between the new moon and the full moon.

Well of Fate: The source of all wisdom, including the one contained in the ancient runes.

Wheel of the Year: One cycle of the seasonal year, consisting of eight seasons.

Younger Futhark: A simplified version of the original runic alphabet developed during the Viking Age.

Zodiac: A circle divided into 12 equal sectors of 30 degrees represented by the zodiac signs and houses.

Conclusion

Divination is an ancient art that has been used for centuries for various purposes. It can be used in magic or just as a guide for spiritual growth. One of the oldest divination methods is astrology - the art of discerning the future by looking at the sky. Astrology associates earthly events with the positions and movements of celestial bodies, including the sun, the moon, the planets, and stellar constellations. These bodies are linked to the 12 zodiac houses, which are shown by the Earth's 24-hour trip around its orbit, and the 12 zodiac signs, which are shown by the sun's path around the Earth every year.

Numerology is another well-known method, which is the art of working out a person's life path from their numbers. Apart from carrying a magical meaning, numbers also have planetary correspondences. Adding together the numbers that make up your date of birth - year, month, and day - you can better decipher the secrets hidden within you. This is similar to looking at the positions and movements of the planets.

The most commonly used divination method is tarot. However, contrary to popular belief, tarot cards won't help you predict the future. They only offer a general guideline for future outcomes. How you interpret them is up to you - and the forces affecting your work. The secret to its popularity is twofold. You can use it to increase self-awareness and reflect on your values and life, answer someone else's questions, or simply for developing your intuition.

Another benefit of tarot is that there are numerous spreads you can choose from.

Palmistry, or chiromancy, is another divination technique practiced by several ancient civilizations. In palmistry, you're looking into someone's hand to explore their personality traits to determine how their characteristics, thoughts, emotions, and actions may affect their future. Each hand is associated with different brain activities, and each line on one's hand is an expression of these activities. Since most activities are the result of your core personality, interpreting them can give you an insight into how your future may unfold.

Runes are symbols of different magical properties. Traditionally, runes are engraved on wood or stone - although they can also be written on a piece of paper or painted on a talisman to be carried with you. Engraved runes are carried in a protective bag. When needed, they are tossed out, and questions asked, generally about future events. As in the case of tarot cards, the runes facing up carry the most likely answers. Written runes are typically used for protection, reflection, or drawing in positive forces.

Similar to runes, crystals also have magical properties. They can soak in both positive and negative energy. Lithomancy, or divination with crystals and stones, is also a more accurate method to discern the future. Crystals can be used alone or in a grid, harnessing their cumulative powers. Crystal ball divination is a specific form of divinatory method. It involves gazing into a crystal ball, asking questions about the future, and interpreting the answers based on the images shown in the ball. It requires deep focus and the ability to eliminate any unrelated thoughts from one's mind to avoid misinterpretation of the messages.

Here's another book by Silvia Hill that you might like

Free Bonus from Silvia Hill available for limited time

Hi Spirituality Lovers!

My name is Silvia Hill, and first off, I want to THANK YOU for reading my book.

Now you have a chance to join my exclusive spirituality email list so you can get the ebooks below for free as well as the potential to get more spirituality ebooks for free! Simply click the link below to join.

P.S. Remember that it's 100% free to join the list.

~~$27~~ **FREE BONUSES**

-  9 Types of Spirit Guides and How to Connect to Them
- 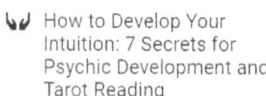 How to Develop Your Intuition: 7 Secrets for Psychic Development and Tarot Reading
- 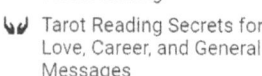 Tarot Reading Secrets for Love, Career, and General Messages

Access your free bonuses here
https://livetolearn.lpages.co/divination-for-beginners/

References

Davis-Holmes, K. (2019, March 7). Most Commonly Used Divination Techniques. Woman on Thin Ice. https://kateonthinice.com/10-most-commonly-used-divination-techniques/

WiseWitch. (2018, April 11). Divination: Types and practices. Wise Witches and Witchcraft. https://witchcraftandwitches.com/divination-fortune-telling/divination-types-and-practices/

Dean, L. (2019). The divination handbook: The modern seer's guide to using tarot, crystals, palmistry, and more. Fair Winds Press.

Divination. (2012). In Introduction to Cultural Mathematics (pp. 103-122). John Wiley & Sons, Inc.

Divination: We all just want to know what's coming next. (2018, January 24). Psychology Today. https://www.psychologytoday.com/intl/blog/myth-the-mind/201801/divination-we-all-just-want-know-what-s-coming-next

Nami's guide to crystal divination/crystal throwing. (n.d.). Tumblr https://themanicnami.tumblr.com/post/150142807211/namis-guide-to-crystal-divinationcrystal

Park, G. K., & Gilbert, R. A. (2001). divination. In Encyclopedia Britannica.

Robertson, D. (n.d.). Divination as storytelling: Dealing (with) death and extinction. Open.ac.uk. http://www.open.ac.uk/blogs/religious-studies/?p=1202

Santo, D. E. (2019). Divination. Cambridge Encyclopedia of Anthropology. https://www.anthroencyclopedia.com/entry/divination

The Editors of Encyclopedia Britannica. (2007). crystal gazing. In Encyclopedia Britannica.

Tuczay, C. A. (2015). Magic and Divination. In Set Handbook of Medieval Culture. DE GRUYTER.

Wigington, P. (2010a, January 27). Reading the stones for divination. Learn Religions. https://www.learnreligions.com/divination-with-stones-2561751

Wigington, P. (2010b, September 20). Learn about the basics of numerology. Learn Religions. https://www.learnreligions.com/the-basics-of-numerology-2561761

Wigington, P. (2012, April 4). Methods of Divination. Learn Religions. https://www.learnreligions.com/methods-of-divination-2561764

Wigington, P. (2013, October 12). Bone Divination. Learn Religions. https://www.learnreligions.com/bone-divination-2562499

Wiśniewski, R. (n.d.). Christian divination in late antiquity – Bryn Mawr Classical Review. Brynmawr.edu. https://bmcr.brynmawr.edu/2021/2021.12.13/

Gulino, E. (2020, June 25). There Are 80+ Types Of Astrology. Here's Where To Start. Refinery29.Com; Refinery29. https://www.refinery29.com/en-us/types-of-astrology

Astrology vs Astronomy: What's the Difference? (2014, July 14). Sky & Telescope. https://skyandtelescope.org/astronomy-resources/whats-difference-astrology-vs-astronomy/

Brown, M. (n.d.). What Is Astrology, Actually? InStyle https://www.instyle.com/lifestyle/astrology/what-is-astrology

How You Can Predict Your Future Using Astrology? (n.d.). Streetdirectory.Com. 2022, from https://www.streetdirectory.com/etoday/-uwcalj.html

Garis, M. G. (2020, December 18). The 5 Most Common Mistakes People Make When Reading Their Horoscope, According to an Astrologer. Well+Good. https://www.wellandgood.com/how-read-horoscope/

Understanding the Astrological Chart Wheel. (2018, March 15). Cafeastrology.Com. https://cafeastrology.com/articles/how-to-understand-read-chart-wheel.html

Astrology Symbols and Glyphs. (2015, April 16). Cafeastrology.Com. https://cafeastrology.com/astrology-symbols-glyphs.html

Hall, M. (n.d.). Understand the Basics of Astrology. LiveAbout. https://www.liveabout.com/what-is-astrology-206723

Brown, M. (2022, July 19). Your astrological birth chart, explained. POPSUGAR. https://www.popsugar.com/smart-living/astrology-birth-chart-48875828

DeSimone, M. (2020, August 20). The benefits of getting a birth chart reading. Tarot.com. https://www.tarot.com/astrology/birth-chart-benefits

Hall, M. (2007, March 4). Scorpio moon sign: Personality and characteristics. LiveAbout. https://www.liveabout.com/scorpio-moon-moon-signs-206988

Williams, M. (2022, March 31). What is a birth chart in astrology? Chani Nicholas. https://chaninicholas.com/what-is-a-birth-chart/

Astrogle. (2010, December 17). Origins of Numerology and its usage. Vedic Astrology & Ayurveda. https://www.astrogle.com/numerology/origins-of-numerology-and-its-usage.html

Beltran, M. A. (2020, July 29). Discover the ancient practice of numerology. Thriveglobal.com. https://thriveglobal.com/stories/discover-the-ancient-practice-of-numerology/

Chaldean Numerology. (2021, October 6). GaneshaSpeaks. https://www.ganeshaspeaks.com/numerology/types/chaldean/

Ducie, S. (2017). What is numerology? ReadHowYouWant.com.

Elementually. (2022, April 25). The combined power of astrology and numerology. Witchy Spiritual Stuff. https://witchyspiritualstuff.com/astrology-and-numerology-combined/

History of Numerology. (2021, June 4). MyPandit. https://www.mypandit.com/numerology/history/

History Of Numerology. (2021, October 6). GaneshaSpeaks. https://www.ganeshaspeaks.com/numerology/history/

Hurst, K. (2017, December 18). Numerology: What is Numerology & how does it work? The Law Of Attraction; Cosmic Media LLC. https://thelawofattraction.com/what-is-numerology/

Jain, S. (2022, June 8). Types of numerology number systems and their interpretation. AstroTalk Blog - Online Astrology Consultation with Astrologer; AstroTalk. https://astrotalk.com/astrology-blog/types-of-numerology-number-systems-and-their-interpretation/

Luke. (2020, December 27). How does numerology work with astrology? MIND IS THE MASTER. https://mindisthemaster.com/astrology-and-numerology/

Moon, R. W., & Shadow, C. (2020). Numerology and astrology: 2 Books in 1. The complete collection of books on numerology and astrology for beginners. Includes relationships and dating compatibility, zodiac signs and horoscope. Rdl Publishing.

www.ingramcontent.com/pod-product-compliance
Lightning Source LLC
Chambersburg PA
CBHW070336010526
44107CB00004B/523